OPPOSING
VIEWPOINTS®
SERIES

Hacking and Hackers

Other Books of Related Interest

Opposing Viewpoints Series

Cybercrime
Internet Censorship
Netiquette and Online Ethics

At Issue Series

Policing the Internet
Technology and the Cloud
Wikileaks

Current Controversies Series

E-books
Internet Activism
Mobile Apps

"Congress shall make
no law ... abridging
the freedom of speech,
or of the press."

First Amendment to the US Constitution

The basic foundation of our democracy is the First Amendment guarantee of freedom of expression. The Opposing Viewpoints Series is dedicated to the concept of this basic freedom and the idea that it is more important to practice it than to enshrine it.

OPPOSING
VIEWPOINTS®
SERIES

Hacking and Hackers

Margaret Haerens and Lynn M. Zott, Book Editors

GREENHAVEN PRESS
A part of Gale, Cengage Learning

GALE
CENGAGE Learning·

Detroit • New York • San Francisco • New Haven. Conn • Waterville. Maine • London

GALE
CENGAGE Learning·

Elizabeth Des Chenes, *Director, Content Strategy*
Cynthia Sanner, *Publisher*
Douglas Dentino, *Manager, New Product*

© 2014 Greenhaven Press, a part of Gale, Cengage Learning

Articles in Greenhaven Press anthologies are often edited for length to meet page requirements. In addition, original titles of these works are changed to clearly present the main thesis and to explicitly indicate the author's opinion. Every effort is made to ensure that Greenhaven Press accurately reflects the original intent of the authors. Every effort has been made to trace the owners of copyrighted material.

Cover Image © pogonici/Shutterstock.com.

LIBRARY OF CONGRESS CATALOGING-IN-PUBLICATION DATA

Hacking and hackers / Margaret Haerens and Lynn M. Zott, book editors.
    pages cm. -- (Opposing viewpoints)
    Includes bibliographical references and index.
    ISBN 978-0-7377-6656-1 (hardcover) -- ISBN 978-0-7377-6657-8 (pbk.)
  1. Computer crimes. 2. Computer hackers. 3. Hacktivism. I. Haerens, Margaret.
II. Zott, Lynn M. (Lynn Marie), 1969-
    HV6773.H33 2013
    364.16'8--dc23
                                                                            2013009181

Printed in the United States of America
    1 2 3 4 5   17 16 15 14 13

Contents

Why Consider Opposing Viewpoints?   11

Introduction   14

Chapter 1: What Is the Most Effective Way to Combat Hacking?

Chapter Preface   19

1. A Clear and Unified Approach Is Needed to Ensure Cybersecurity   21
   Mike McConnell

2. Hackers Are Not a Threat to Cybersecurity   28
   James Andrew Lewis

3. US Outgunned in Hacker War   37
   Devlin Barrett

4. A Multifaceted Strategy Is Best to Ensure Cybersecurity   43
   Michael P. Merritt

5. Private Sector Isn't Waiting for Feds to Deal with Internet Security   57
   John Hayward

6. Ethical Hacking Improves Cybersecurity   63
   Sue Marquette Poremba

7. Exploding the Myth of the "Ethical Hacker"   67
   Conrad Constantine and Dominique Karg

Periodical and Internet Sources Bibliography   73

Chapter 2: Is Hacktivism a Serious Threat?

Chapter Preface   75

1. Hacktivism Is an Effective and Ethical Means of Social Protest   77
   Graham Armstrong

2. Hacktivist Collectives Are Terrorists   83
   Phil Elmore

3. Hacktivists Fight for Civil Liberties and Free Expression 88
   James Ball

4. Old-Time Hacktivists: Anonymous, You've Crossed
   the Line   97
   Elinor Mills

Periodical and Internet Sources Bibliography   104

Chapter 3: What Is the Significance of WikiLeaks?

Chapter Preface   106

1. WikiLeaks Provides Transparency and Can Deter
   Corporate and Government Misbehavior   109
   Jesse Walker

2. The WikiLeaks Scandal Reveals the Limitations of
   the Public's Desire for Transparency   114
   Alasdair Roberts

3. WikiLeaks Is an Unprecedented Threat to US
   National Security   127
   Marc A. Thiessen

4. A Defense of Wikileaks   132
   John B. Judis

5. The WikiLeaks Scandal Reveals the US Government
   Lacks the Will to Deal with Cyberthreats   138
   Cliff May

Periodical and Internet Sources Bibliography   143

Chapter 4: What Is the Role of Government in Hacking?

Chapter Preface   145

1. Cyberattacks Require a Military Response   148
   US Department of Defense

2. A Military Response to Cyberattacks Is Unwarranted and Inappropriate 153
Benjamin H. Friedman and Christopher Preble

3. The United States Needs to Develop a Smart and Effective Counterinsurgency Strategy for Cyberspace 159
Paul Rosenzweig

4. More Government Regulation Would Impede Innovation and Cybersecurity 171
Tom Ridge

5. The United States Should Engage in Cyberwarfare Treaty Talks 180
Alice Slater

Periodical and Internet Sources Bibliography 186

For Further Discussion 187

Organizations to Contact 189

Bibliography of Books 196

Index 200

Why Consider Opposing Viewpoints?

> "The only way in which a human being can make some approach to knowing the whole of a subject is by hearing what can be said about it by persons of every variety of opinion and studying all modes in which it can be looked at by every character of mind. No wise man ever acquired his wisdom in any mode but this."
>
> John Stuart Mill

In our media-intensive culture it is not difficult to find differing opinions. Thousands of newspapers and magazines and dozens of radio and television talk shows resound with differing points of view. The difficulty lies in deciding which opinion to agree with and which "experts" seem the most credible. The more inundated we become with differing opinions and claims, the more essential it is to hone critical reading and thinking skills to evaluate these ideas. Opposing Viewpoints books address this problem directly by presenting stimulating debates that can be used to enhance and teach these skills. The varied opinions contained in each book examine many different aspects of a single issue. While examining these conveniently edited opposing views, readers can develop critical thinking skills such as the ability to compare and contrast authors' credibility, facts, argumentation styles, use of persuasive techniques, and other stylistic tools. In short, the Opposing Viewpoints Series is an ideal way to attain the higher-level thinking and reading skills so essential in a culture of diverse and contradictory opinions.

In addition to providing a tool for critical thinking, Opposing Viewpoints books challenge readers to question their own strongly held opinions and assumptions. Most people form their opinions on the basis of upbringing, peer pressure, and personal, cultural, or professional bias. By reading carefully balanced opposing views, readers must directly confront new ideas as well as the opinions of those with whom they disagree. This is not to argue simplistically that everyone who reads opposing views will—or should—change his or her opinion. Instead, the series enhances readers' understanding of their own views by encouraging confrontation with opposing ideas. Careful examination of others' views can lead to the readers' understanding of the logical inconsistencies in their own opinions, perspective on why they hold an opinion, and the consideration of the possibility that their opinion requires further evaluation.

Evaluating Other Opinions

To ensure that this type of examination occurs, Opposing Viewpoints books present all types of opinions. Prominent spokespeople on different sides of each issue as well as well-known professionals from many disciplines challenge the reader. An additional goal of the series is to provide a forum for other, less known, or even unpopular viewpoints. The opinion of an ordinary person who has had to make the decision to cut off life support from a terminally ill relative, for example, may be just as valuable and provide just as much insight as a medical ethicist's professional opinion. The editors have two additional purposes in including these less known views. One, the editors encourage readers to respect others' opinions—even when not enhanced by professional credibility. It is only by reading or listening to and objectively evaluating others' ideas that one can determine whether they are worthy of consideration. Two, the inclusion of such viewpoints encourages the important critical thinking skill of objectively evaluating an author's credentials and bias. This evaluation will illuminate an author's reasons for taking a particular stance on an issue and will aid in readers' evaluation of the author's ideas.

It is our hope that these books will give readers a deeper understanding of the issues debated and an appreciation of the complexity of even seemingly simple issues when good and honest people disagree. This awareness is particularly important in a democratic society such as ours in which people enter into public debate to determine the common good. Those with whom one disagrees should not be regarded as enemies but rather as people whose views deserve careful examination and may shed light on one's own.

Thomas Jefferson once said that "difference of opinion leads to inquiry, and inquiry to truth." Jefferson, a broadly educated man, argued that "if a nation expects to be ignorant and free . . . it expects what never was and never will be." As individuals and as a nation, it is imperative that we consider the opinions of others and examine them with skill and discernment. The Opposing Viewpoints Series is intended to help readers achieve this goal.

David L. Bender and Bruno Leone,
Founders

Introduction

> "If EVERYONE could interact with
> computers with the same innocent,
> productive, creative impulse that
> hackers did, the Hacker Ethic
> might spread through society like a
> benevolent ripple, and computers
> would indeed change the world for
> the better."
>
> Steven Levy, Hackers: Heroes of
> the Computer Revolution, 1984

> "While the vast majority of hackers
> may be disinclined towards violence,
> it would only take a few to turn cyber
> terrorism into reality."
>
> Dorothy E. Denning, Social
> Science Research Council essay,
> November 1, 2001

In June 1903 John Ambrose Fleming, a British physicist and engineer, performed a demonstration of the latest radio technology—the wireless telegraph—at the prestigious Royal Institution in London. Developed by the celebrated Italian inventor Guglielmo Marconi, the wireless telegraph sent messages across long distances by Morse code. During the highly-anticipated demonstration, Marconi would transmit a coded message to Fleming from another wireless telegraph nearly 300 miles away in Cornwall, England. Marconi and Fleming aimed to showcase the state-of-the-art technology to the best and brightest of London's scientific and engineering community.

Before the demonstration was set to begin, however, the telegraph furiously began to type out one word repeatedly: "Rats!" It then transcribed a poem: "There was a young fellow of Italy / who diddled the public quite prettily." The lecture hall erupted, and both Marconi and Fleming were outraged and embarrassed. Marconi had bragged that the wireless telegraph was a completely secure technology, and he had been proven wrong in front of a number of amused colleagues. It was also one of the first cases of hacking in recorded history.

Four days later, the hacker revealed himself in a letter to *The Times*, an English newspaper. Its author was Nevil Maskelyne, a British hall musician and inventor frustrated with Marconi's patents on wireless technology, which hindered his own work in that area. His hacking not only got revenge and publicity but revealed flaws in the technology that could comprise transmissions and intercept supposedly secure messages.

Computer hacking can be traced back to the 1960s when a group of model-train enthusiasts at the Massachusetts Institute of Technology became interested in the large mainframe computers installed at the university. Calling themselves hackers, a term that they had invented after hacking their electronic trains and switches to improve their performance, they began to experiment with and modify computer programs to customize them for specific applications or investigate how they were put together. They formulated shortcuts and improvements of their own, creating more efficient programs in many cases. At that time, hacker was a positive term that described a resourceful person who displayed impressive computer programming skills. For years, hacking was limited to a small group of computer enthusiasts, because computers were not available to the general public.

It wasn't until the 1980s and the proliferation of personal computers that hacking became a widespread practice. As individuals purchased computers and set up modems to communicate with other computers over telephone lines, the potential for motivated, curious, and resourceful people to play with the technology skyrocketed. Electronic bulletin boards allowed hackers to post tips on how to gain access to protected networks and share stolen computer passwords. In 1983 the film *War Games* popularized the idea of hacking. The film followed the exploits of a young hacker who manages to get access to the US government's military supercomputer and almost starts World War III.

In one of the first major cases of computer hacking, a group of six teenagers from Milwaukee who met as members of a local scouting troop found that they had a common interest in hacking. After gaining access to dozens of highly secure and classified computer systems, including Los Alamos National Laboratory and Security Pacific Bank, the group, known as the 414s (a term referring to their local area code) were identified and caught by the FBI in 1983. The case garnered national interest and widespread media coverage.

Hackers began to form collectives and coordinate cyberattacks on other hackers as well as corporate and government websites through denial-of-service (DoS) attacks, in which one or more people can overload a web server by bombarding it with external communication requests. Among the first collectives were the Legion of Doom in the United States and Chaos Computer Club in Germany.

By the mid-1980s, hacking was also a criminal enterprise. Hackers began to access computer systems and classified information for personal gain, stealing credit card numbers and pirating software and games. Traditional hackers began to call these individuals "crackers," and they also became known as "black hat" hackers. Hackers employed to assess computer security systems in order to protect it against "black hat" hackers are known as "white hat" or ethical hackers.

As criminal hacking increased, governments began to address the growing problem. The US Congress passed its first antihacking legislation, the Computer Fraud and Abuse Act, in 1986. The law gave federal authorities more power to prosecute and punish hacking by making it a felony crime. Law enforcement also became more aggressive in investigating and prosecuting criminal hackers, making a number of high-profile arrests and prosecutions.

Hacktivism also emerged as a powerful force on the Internet. Hacktivists use their skills in support of a political or social movement or to advance a political or social agenda. A recent case of hacktivism is the Arab Spring, when activists on Facebook and Twitter posted citizen videos and attacked government websites in support of pro-democracy movements in the Middle East. Hacktivists have intervened in the gay marriage debate, the Iraq and Afghanistan War, the Syrian Civil War, and other matters.

Nation-states have also gotten in on the act. Hackers associated with governments—whether employed by them or supportive of their policies—have attacked the websites of other nation-states via DoS attacks, computer viruses, or other methods in order to shut down key government services or infrastructure. For countries that perpetrate cyberattacks, it is an effective way to disrupt an opponent's computer systems and do significant damage without launching a military campaign. As cyberattacks have more impact, they are increasingly regarded as national security threats and are threatened with massive retaliation strikes. Many experts believe that cyberwar between nation-states is a real threat and are concerned about the effects of a coordinated cyberattack on a nation's infrastructure.

Hacking continues to evolve as technology improves and the Internet becomes more central to human existence. The authors of the viewpoints in *Opposing Viewpoints: Hacking and Hackers* discuss hacking in the following chapters: What Is the Most Effective Way to Combat Hacking?, Is Hacktivism a Serious Threat?, What Is the Significance of WikiLeaks?, and What Is the Role of Government in Hacking? The viewpoints examine the role of ethical hacking and hacktivism, suggest the most effective way for governments and private industry to respond to hacking, and offer perspectives on the impact of WikiLeaks.

CHAPTER 1

What Is the Most Effective Way to Combat Hacking?

Chapter Preface

In the past few decades, the Internet has become an essential tool in every aspect of business, academia, entertainment, communication, journalism, scientific research, and almost every other human endeavor. As individuals, businesses, organizations, and governments become more dependent on working online, they have also become more vulnerable to hackers who scheme their way into computer networks to steal information, block access to websites and information, or even shut down critical infrastructure and services. To protect information systems, governments and businesses rely on computer security to anticipate and block the efforts of criminal hackers. Ethical hackers are key to this effort, because they assess an organization's cybersecurity, pinpoint vulnerable areas and possible problems, and fortify cyberdefenses.

Ethical hackers, also known as tiger teams, white hats, red teams, or sneakers, perform penetration testing and other testing methodologies to assess the security of an organization's information systems. Penetration testing simulates a malicious cyberattack from criminal hackers—those who have access to vital networks and those who are complete outsiders and have no inside knowledge or security clearances. Ethical hackers look for things like hardware or software flaws and ineffective or delayed responses to a cyberattack. In addition, ethical hackers evaluate the potential damage of a successful cyberattack to the organization and its information systems. The results of the penetration test and the ethical hacker's analysis is then presented to the organization in hopes of addressing the identified problems and strengthening its cybersecurity.

Ethical hacking can be traced back to the early days of the Internet. The first known cases occurred as classified operations in the US military to test the vulnerability of its information systems to hackers. These early penetration tests aimed to better protect US national security from the emerging threat of computer hackers.

As more and more corporations and businesses began to realize the potential of the Internet, it became clear that computer security would also play a central role in the private sector. Two pioneers in the field were Dan Farmer and Wietse Venema, who first explored the idea of utilizing hacker techniques to assess cybersecurity. Their ideas were posted to Usenet, an early Internet forum, in December 1993. In this legendary post, Farmer and Venema described their ethical hacking attempts, providing specific examples of how they were able to access computer networks and suggesting ways to effectively counter such attacks in the future.

Farmer and Venema recognized that computer security would be key to the Internet's growth and effectiveness. They utilized their experiences and knowledge and developed the Security Administrator Tool for Analyzing Networks (SATAN), a tool designed for systems administrators to test their own cybersecurity. In 1995 Farmer and Venema posted the SATAN application for anyone to download for free.

The release of SATAN proved highly controversial. Some people believed that the application was an automatic hacker program that would immediately attack their computer systems as soon as it was downloaded. Others saw a danger in publicizing hacker techniques, thinking that it would encourage people to take up cyberattacks. Yet most systems administrators recognized the value in a practical tool that helped them evaluate and strengthen their organization's cyberdefenses.

The field of ethical hacking would develop quickly in the following few decades. Its role is explored in the following chapter, which examines the best ways to combat hacking, the role of private companies, and the most effective cyberstrategies.

"The cyber-war mirrors the nuclear challenge in terms of the potential economic and psychological effects."

A Clear and Unified Approach Is Needed to Ensure Cybersecurity

Mike McConnell

Mike McConnell is the former director of the National Security Agency and executive vice president of Booz Allen Hamilton. In the following viewpoint, he claims the United States is fighting a cyberwar and losing. McConnell argues that the US government must formulate a clear and unified response to the threat. An essential component of the strategy, he insists, should be a productive collaboration with private industry that spans international law, privacy and civil liberties, and security concerns. Officials can also look to the Cold War to learn from past efforts, McConnell explains, concluding that such an initiative will be key to winning the cyberwar and protecting US national security.

As you read, consider the following questions:

1. According to NetWitness, how many companies worldwide were compromised in a sophisticated cyberattack launched in 2008?

2. What percentage of the physical infrastructure of the web does the author say is owned by private industry?

3. What year was Project Solarium launched, according to the viewpoint?

The United States is fighting a cyber-war today, and we are losing. It's that simple. As the most wired nation on Earth, we offer the most targets of significance, yet our cyber-defenses are woefully lacking.

Developing a Cohesive Strategy

The problem is not one of resources; even in our current fiscal straits, we can afford to upgrade our defenses. The problem is that we lack a cohesive strategy to meet this challenge.

The stakes are enormous. To the extent that the sprawling U.S. economy inhabits a common physical space, it is in our communications networks. If an enemy disrupted our financial and accounting transactions, our equities and bond markets or our retail commerce—or created confusion about the legitimacy of those transactions—chaos would result. Our power grids, air and ground transportation, telecommunications, and water-filtration systems are in jeopardy as well.

These battles are not hypothetical. Google's networks were hacked in an attack that began in December [2009] and that the company said emanated from China. And recently the security firm NetWitness reported that more than 2,500 companies worldwide were compromised in a sophisticated attack launched in 2008 and aimed at proprietary corporate data. Indeed, the recent Cyber Shock Wave simulation revealed what those of us involved in national security policy have long feared: For all our war games and strategy documents focused on traditional warfare, we have yet to address the most basic questions about cyber-conflicts.

Lessons from the Cold War

What is the right strategy for this most modern of wars? Look to history. During the Cold War, when the United States faced an existential threat from the Soviet Union, we relied on deterrence to protect ourselves from nuclear attack. Later, as the East-West stalemate ended and nuclear weapons proliferated, some argued that preemption made more sense in an age of global terrorism.

The cyber-war mirrors the nuclear challenge in terms of the potential economic and psychological effects. So, should our strategy be deterrence or preemption? The answer: both. Depending on the nature of the threat, we can deploy aspects of either approach to defend America in cyberspace.

During the Cold War, deterrence was based on a few key elements: attribution (understanding who attacked us), location (knowing where a strike came from), response (being able to respond, even if attacked first) and transparency (the enemy's knowledge of our capability and intent to counter with massive force).

Against the Soviets, we dealt with the attribution and location challenges by developing human intelligence behind the Iron Curtain and by fielding early-warning radar systems, reconnaissance satellites and undersea listening posts to monitor threats. We invested heavily in our response capabilities with intercontinental ballistic missiles, submarines and long-range bombers, as well as command-and-control systems and specialized staffs to run them. The resources available were commensurate with the challenge at hand—as must be the case in cyberspace.

Practical Policies Are Fundamental

Just as important was the softer side of our national security strategy: the policies, treaties and diplomatic efforts that underpinned containment and deterrence. Our alliances, such as NATO [North Atlantic Treaty Organization], made clear that a strike on one would be a strike on all and would be met with massive retaliation. This unambiguous intent, together with our ability to monitor and respond, provided a credible nuclear deterrent that served us well.

How do we apply deterrence in the cyber-age? For one, we must clearly express our intent. Secretary of State Hillary Rodham Clinton offered a succinct statement to that effect last month in Washington, [DC,] in a speech on Internet freedom. "Countries or individuals that engage in cyber-attacks should face consequences and international condemnation," she said. "In an Internet-connected world, an attack on one nation's networks can be an attack on all."

That was a promising move, but it means little unless we back it up with practical policies and international legal agreements to define norms and identify consequences for destructive behavior in cyberspace. We began examining these issues through the Comprehensive National Cybersecurity Initiative, launched during the George W. Bush administration, but more work is needed on outlining how, when and where we would respond to an attack. For now, we have a response mechanism in name only.

Developing the Right Technology

The United States must also translate our intent into capabilities. We need to develop an early-warning system to monitor cyberspace, identify intrusions and locate the source of attacks with a trail of evidence that can support diplomatic, military and legal options—and we must be able to do this in milliseconds. More specifically, we need to reengineer the Internet to make attribution, geolocation, intelligence analysis and impact assessment— who did it, from where, why and what was the result—more manageable. The technologies are already available from public and private sources and can be further developed if we have the will to build them into our systems and to work with our allies and trading partners so they will do the same.

Of course, deterrence can be effective when the enemy is a state with an easily identifiable government and location. It is less successful against criminal groups or extremists who cannot

Internet Security Needs to Be Strengthened Worldwide

Governments and citizens must have confidence that the networks at the core of their national security and economic prosperity are safe and resilient. Now this is about more than petty hackers who deface websites. Our ability to bank online, use electronic commerce, and safeguard billions of dollars in intellectual property are all at stake if we cannot rely on the security of our information networks.

Disruptions in these systems demand a coordinated response by all governments, the private sector, and the international community. We need more tools to help law enforcement agencies cooperate across jurisdictions when criminal hackers and organized crime syndicates attack networks for financial gain. The same is true when social ills such as child pornography and the exploitation of trafficked women and girls online is there for the world to see and for those who exploit these people to make a profit. We applaud efforts such as the Council on Europe's Convention on Cybercrime that facilitate international cooperation in prosecuting such offenses. And we wish to redouble our efforts.

Hillary Clinton, "Remarks on Internet Freedom," January 21, 2010. www.state.gov.

be readily traced, let alone deterred through sanctions or military action.

Devising Preemptive Strategies

There are many organizations (including al-Qaeda) that are not motivated by greed, as with criminal organizations, or a desire for geopolitical advantage, as with many states. Rather, their worldview seeks to destroy the systems of global commerce, trade and travel that are undergirded by our cyber-infrastructure. So deterrence is not enough; preemptive strategies might be required before such adversaries launch a devastating cyber-attack.

We preempt such groups by degrading, interdicting and eliminating their leadership and capabilities to mount cyber-attacks, and by creating a more resilient cyberspace that can absorb attacks and quickly recover. To this end, we must hammer out a consensus on how to best harness the capabilities of the National Security Agency [NSA], which I had the privilege to lead from 1992 to 1996. The NSA is the only agency in the United States with the legal authority, oversight and budget dedicated to breaking the codes and understanding the capabilities and intentions of potential enemies. The challenge is to shape an effective partnership with the private sector so information can move quickly back and forth from public to private—and classified to unclassified—to protect the nation's critical infrastructure.

We must give key private-sector leaders (from the transportation, utility and financial arenas) access to information on emerging threats so they can take countermeasures. For this to work, the private sector needs to be able to share network information—on a controlled basis—without inviting lawsuits from shareholders and others.

Collaboration Is Essential

Obviously, such measures must be contemplated very carefully. But the reality is that while the lion's share of cybersecurity expertise lies in the federal government, more than 90 percent of the physical infrastructure of the Web is owned by private industry. Neither side on its own can mount the cyber-defense we need; some collaboration is inevitable. Recent reports of a possible partnership between Google and the government point to the kind of joint efforts—and shared challenges—that we are likely to see in the future.

No doubt, such arrangements will muddy the waters between the traditional roles of the government and the private sector. We must define the parameters of such interactions, but we should not dismiss them. Cyberspace knows no borders, and our defensive efforts must be similarly seamless.

Shaping a Unified Approach

Ultimately, to build the right strategy to defend cyberspace, we need the equivalent of President Dwight D. Eisenhower's Project Solarium. That 1953 initiative brought together teams of experts with opposing views to develop alternative strategies on how to wage the Cold War. The teams presented their views to the president, and Eisenhower chose his preferred approach—deterrence. We now need a dialogue among business, civil society and government on the challenges we face in cyberspace—spanning international law, privacy and civil liberties, security, and the architecture of the Internet. The results should shape our cybersecurity strategy.

We prevailed in the Cold War through strong leadership, clear policies, solid alliances and close integration of our diplomatic, economic and military efforts. We backed all this up with robust investments—security never comes cheap. It worked, because we had to make it work.

Let's do the same with cybersecurity. The time to start was yesterday.

> *"Only by adapting an exceptionally elastic definition of cyber attack can we say they are frequent."*

Hackers Are Not a Threat to Cybersecurity

James Andrew Lewis

James Andrew Lewis is the director and senior fellow in the Technology and Public Policy Program at the Center for Strategic and International Studies. In the following viewpoint, he asserts that the threat of a true cyberwar is exaggerated and that there have only been two to three cyberattacks since the birth of the Internet. Lewis suggests that what people think are cyberattacks are little more than annoyances, and that in fact, a true cyberattack should result in major physical damage or casualties. Only a few countries have the technological capability to launch a cyberattack, he insists, but it is widely accepted that cyberwarfare will be a part of major conflicts in the future. Limited deterrence may work against conventional enemies, Lewis argues, but terrorist groups or rogue nations may be the biggest threats if they were ever to obtain the capability of cyberattacks.

James Andrew Lewis, "Cyber Attacks, Real or Imagined, and Cyber War," Center for Strategic and International Studies, July 11, 2011. © 2011 by CSIS Publications. All rights reserved. Reproduced by permission.

As you read, consider the following questions:

1. Who does Lewis hold responsible for the cyberattacks against Georgian websites in 2008?
2. How many countries does Lewis believe have advanced cyberattack capabilities?
3. According to Lewis, what did the US Single Integrated Operations Plan do?

A ssorted "cyber attacks" have attracted much attention in the past few months. One headline in this genre recently proclaimed "Anonymous Declares War on Orlando." This is wrong on so many levels that it almost defies analysis. A more precise accounting would show that there have been no cyber wars and perhaps two or three cyber attacks since the Internet first appeared.

The most ironic example of hyperbole catching itself involves the new Department of Defense Cyber Strategy, which says that the United States reserves the right to use military force in response to a cyber attack. Since many reports call everything—pranks, embarrassing leaks, fraud, bank robbery, and espionage—a cyber attack, the strategy led to expressions of concern that the United States would be shooting missiles at annoying teenage hackers or starting wars over WikiLeaks. In fact, the strategy sets a very high threshold that is derived from the laws of armed conflict for defining a cyber attack. Nothing we have seen this year [2011] would qualify as an attack using this threshold.

Cyberwar Is an Exaggerated Threat

Only by adopting an exceptionally elastic definition of cyber attack can we say they are frequent. There have been many annoyances, much crime, and rampant spying, but the only incidents that have caused physical damage or disruption to critical services are the alleged Israeli use of cyber attack to disrupt Syrian air defenses and the Stuxnet attacks against Iran's nuclear facilities. An extortion attempt in Brazil against a public utility may have backfired and temporarily disrupted electrical service. A better way to identify an attack is to rely on "equivalence," where we judge whether a cyber exploit is an attack by asking if it led to physical damage or casualties. No damage, no casualties, means no attack.

Many militaries are developing attack capabilities, but this is not some revolutionary and immensely destructive new form of warfare that any random citizen or hacker can engage in at will. Nations are afraid of cyber war and are careful to stay below the threshold of what could be considered under international law the use of force or an act of war. Crime, even if state sponsored, does not justify a military response. Countries do not go to war over espionage. There is intense hostile activity in cyberspace, but it stays below the threshold of attack.

Examining the Exploits Against Estonia and Georgia

The denial-of-service efforts against Estonian and Georgian websites in 2007 and 2008 were not attacks. The Estonian incident had a clear coercive purpose, and it is worth considering whether the denial-of-service exploit against Estonia could have become the equivalent of an attack if it had been extended in scope and duration. The exploits against Georgia, while undertaken with coercive intent and closely coordinated with Russian military activities (and a useful indicator of how Russia will use cyber warfare), did no damage other than to deface government websites.

The recent escapades involving groups like Anonymous or Lulzsec do not qualify as attacks. Anonymous and Lulzsec did not disrupt critical operations of the companies or agencies they struck. There was embarrassment, but no damage, destruction, or casualties. These were political actions—cyber demonstrations and graffiti—spun up by media attention and copycatting.

Information Is a Weapon

Some nations—Russia in particular—argue that political actions are in fact the core of the new kind of warfare, and the issue is really "information warfare" rather than "cyber warfare." They have said that information is a weapon and that the United States will exploit the Internet to destabilize governments it opposes. Information is a threat to authoritarian regimes, and they want to limit access to websites and social networks. This effort to extend cyber attack to include access to information, however, makes little sense. It distorts long-standing ideas on warfare and military action by disconnecting them from the concept of the use of armed force and violence. The use of force produces immediate physical harm and is central to defining attack and warfare. The concept is incorporated in elements of the UN [United Nations] Charter and the Hague and Geneva Conventions. Publishing or sharing an idea is not the use of force. Though an expanded definition of warfare may serve the political interests of authoritarian regimes, it is not an accurate description of military action or attack.

There are countries that could launch damaging cyber attacks. At least 5 militaries have advanced cyber-attack capabilities, and at least another 30 countries intend to acquire them. These high-end opponents have the resources and skills to overcome most defenses. Just as only a few countries had aircraft in 1914 but most militaries had acquired them 10 years later, every military will eventually acquire some level of cyber-attack capability. Cyber attacks will likely be used only in combination with other military actions, but they will be part of any future conflict. We can regard them as another weapons system with both tactical and strategic uses, similar to missiles or aircraft that can be launched from a distance and strike rapidly at a target.

Investigating the Effects of Cyberattacks

Stuxnet, for example, was a "military grade" cyber exploit and a precisely targeted alternative to an airstrike on Iranian nuclear facilities. It did less damage than an air attack but avoided distressing photos of burning buildings and claims of civilian casualties. The political effect on the Iranian people was negligible, while an airstrike would have prompted an emotional reaction. Military planners now have an additional system to consider in their portfolio of weapons and attacks, which offers a new and attractive combination of effect and risk.

The Aurora test at the Idaho National Labs and the Stuxnet worm show that cyber attacks are capable of doing physical damage. Leading cyber powers have carried out network reconnaissance against critical infrastructure in preparation for such attacks. But these infrastructures are the most dangerous form of attack, and therefore hold the most risk for the attacker. At the onset of conflict, attacks that seek to disrupt and confuse are more likely than infrastructure attacks. Cyber warfare will begin with the disruption of crucial networks and data and seek to create uncertainty and doubt among opposing commanders. The goal will be to increase the Clausewitzian "fog of war." This "informational" aspect of cyber war, where an opponent might scramble or erase data or insert false information to mislead an opponent, is a new and powerful military tool.

Learning from the Battle of Britain

The Battle of Britain is a historical example of this kind of warfare. If the Germans had first destroyed the relatively simple network of sensors, control facilities, and communications systems used by Royal Air Force Fighter Command to maneuver defending aircraft, it would have seriously degraded British air capabilities and made ultimate success much more likely. They did not because they did not fully realize how warfare had changed to emphasize the importance of these intangible assets. Exploiting signals, data, and communications had become essential for military superiority. Future warfare between advanced opponents will begin with efforts to degrade command and control, manipulate opponent data, and misinform and confuse commanders (accompanied by electronic warfare actions, along with kinetic strikes on communications networks and perhaps satellites). Cyber exploits will be the opening salvo and a short-notice warning of impending kinetic attack.

Identifying Strategic Targets

Strikes on critical infrastructure carry a higher degree of risk for the attacker if they are used against targets outside the theater of military operations or in the opponent's homeland. An attack on the networks of a deployed military force is to be expected. Attacks on civilian targets in the opponent's homeland are another matter and may escalate any conflict. Military planning will need to consider when it is beneficial to launch cyber attacks that damage critical infrastructure in order to strain and distract the opposing political leadership, and when it is better to limit any cyber strikes to military targets in theater.

This is one area where cyber attack, because of its global reach, may resemble nuclear war. Just as the U.S. Single Integrated Operations Plan and other documents listed and prioritized targets for nuclear weapons, based on satellite and other forms of reconnaissance, an astute cyber planner will identify and prioritize targets for cyber strikes under different conflict scenarios.

Assessing the Damage

A full-blown, no-holds-barred cyber attack against critical infrastructure and networks might be able to reproduce the damage wrought by Hurricane Katrina, with crucial services knocked out and regional economic activity severely curtailed. While Katrina brought immense suffering and hardship, it did not degrade U.S. military capabilities and would not have led to a U.S. defeat. Multiple, simultaneous Katrinas would still not guarantee victory and could risk being seen as an existential threat that would justify a harsh kinetic response. There are many examples of militaries attacking targets that were irrelevant to success and only inflamed the opponent, so we cannot rule out such attacks

The Emerging Cyber-Industrial Complex

Over the past two years there has been a steady drumbeat of alarmist rhetoric coming out of Washington about potential catastrophic cyberthreats. For example, at a Senate Armed Services Committee hearing last year [2010], Chairman Carl Levin said that "cyberweapons and cyberattacks potentially can be devastating, approaching weapons of mass destruction in their effects." Proposed responses include increased federal spending on cybersecurity and the regulation of private network security practices.

The rhetoric of "cyber doom" employed by proponents of increased federal intervention, however, lacks clear evidence of a serious threat that can be verified by the public. As a result, the United States may be witnessing a bout of threat inflation similar to that seen in the run-up to the Iraq War. Additionally, a cyber-industrial complex is emerging, much like the military-industrial complex of the Cold War. This complex may serve to not only supply cybersecurity solutions to the federal government, but to drum up demand for them as well.

Jerry Brito and Tate Watkins, "Loving the Cyber Bomb? The Dangers of Threat Inflation in Cybersecurity Policy," Mercatus Center Working Paper 11–24, April 2011.

(which could be very appealing to terrorist groups, should they ever acquire the ability to launch them), but no one should believe that this is a decisive new weapon. The only "decisive" weapons ever developed were nuclear weapons, and even then, many would have been needed to overcome an opponent.

Pure cyber war—"keyboard versus keyboard" or "geek versus geek"—is unlikely. Cyber attacks are fast, cheap, and moderately destructive, but no one would plan to fight using only cyber weapons. They are not destructive enough to damage an opponent's will and capacity to resist. Cyber attacks will not be decisive, particularly against a large and powerful opponent. The threat of retaliation that is limited to a cyber response may also not be very compelling. Cyber attack is not much of a deterrent.

The Threat of Deterrence

Deterrence uses the implied threat of a damaging military response to keep an opponent from attacking. "Cross-domain" deterrence (where a cyber attack could result in a kinetic response) works at some levels—no nation would launch a cyber-only attack against the United States because of the threat of retaliation. But deterrence does not stop espionage or crime because these actions do not justify the use of military force in response. Since our opponents stay below the threshold of war, this limits what we can "deter."

In the future, even this limited deterrence may not work against terrorist groups or irresponsible nations like Iran or North Korea. For nonstate actors, such as terrorists, it is hard to make a credible threat, since they lack cities and infrastructure to hold hostage and can be willing to commit suicide in an attack. Nations such as Iran and North Korea may have a very different calculation of acceptable risk, being willing to do things that strike other nations as insanely risky (as when North Korea torpedoed a South Korean patrol boat). Iran, North Korea, and others may miscalculate the reactions of the West to a limited cyber attack. When these less deferrable actors acquire advanced cyber capabilities, the likelihood of cyber attack will increase.

A century ago, armies discovered that technology could be the key to victory. Since then there has been a steady stream of new weapons, new technologies, and new ways to attack. Perhaps it is best to see the Internet and cyber attack as the latest in a long line of technologies that have changed warfare and provided new military capabilities. We have only begun to explore the uses of this new capability, and as the world becomes more dependent on networks and computer technology, the value and effect of cyber attack will grow.

> *"In the congressional debate over cybersecurity legislation, the Chamber of Commerce has argued for a voluntary, non-regulatory approach to cybersecurity that would encourage more cooperation . . . between government and business."*

US Outgunned in Hacker War

Devlin Barrett

Devlin Barrett is a reporter for the Wall Street Journal. *In the following viewpoint, he contends that top government security officials believe many corporations fail to recognize the threat posed by criminal hackers and do not adequately protect themselves from cyberattacks. Companies need to rethink the way they use computer networks and be more proactive when it comes to defending their business and their customers' personal information, Barrett argues. One way that companies can do that, he explains, is by aggressively pursuing hackers instead of waiting to be attacked. Another way, he points out, is to develop a comprehensive and unified cyberstrategy.*

As you read, consider the following questions:

1. According to Barrett, how many Sony customers had their personal information compromised by hackers?
2. How many hacking cases does the author say the FBI investigated in 2010?
3. According to Richard Bejtlich, what percentage of companies did not realize that they had been breached by hackers until his security firm told them?

The Federal Bureau of Investigation's top cyber cop offered a grim appraisal of the nation's efforts to keep computer hackers from plundering corporate data networks: "We're not winning," he said.

Shawn Henry, who is preparing to leave the FBI after more than two decades with the bureau, said in an interview that the current public and private approach to fending off hackers is "unsustainable." Computer criminals are simply too talented and defensive measures too weak to stop them, he said.

His comments weren't directed at specific legislation but came as Congress considers two competing measures designed to buttress the networks for critical U.S. infrastructure, such as electrical-power plants and nuclear reactors. Though few cybersecurity experts disagree on the need for security improvements, business advocates have argued that the new regulations called for in one of the bills aren't likely to better protect computer networks.

Mr. Henry, who is leaving government to take a cybersecurity job with an undisclosed firm in Washington, said companies need to make major changes in the way they use computer networks to avoid further damage to national security and the economy. Too many companies, from major multinationals to small start-ups, fail to recognize the financial and legal risks they are taking—or the costs they may have already suffered unknowingly—by operating vulnerable networks, he said.

"I don't see how we ever come out of this without changes in technology or changes in behavior, because with the status quo, it's an unsustainable model. Unsustainable in that you never get ahead, never become secure, never .have a reasonable expectation of privacy or security," Mr. Henry said.

James A. Lewis, a senior fellow on cybersecurity at the Center for Strategic and International Studies, said that as gloomy as Mr. Henry's assessment may sound, "I am actually a little bit gloomier. I think we've lost the opening battle [with hackers]." Mr. Lewis said he didn't believe there was a single secure, unclassified computer network in the U.S.

"There's a kind of willful desire not to admit how bad things are, both in government and certainly in the private sector, so I could see how [Mr. Henry] would be frustrated," he added.

High-profile hacking victims have included Sony Corp., which said last year that hackers had accessed personal information on 24.6 million customers on one of its online game services as part of a broader attack on the company that compromised data on more than 100 million accounts. Nasdaq OMX Group Inc., which operates the Nasdaq Stock Market, also acknowledged last year that hackers had breached a part of its network called Directors Desk, a service for company boards to communicate and share documents. HBGary Federal, a cybersecurity firm, was infiltrated by the hacking collective called Anonymous, which stole tens of thousands of internal emails from the company.

Mr. Henry has played a key role in expanding the FBI's cybersecurity capabilities. In 2002, when the FBI reorganized to put more of its resources toward protecting computer networks, it handled nearly 1,500 hacking cases. Eight years later, that caseload had grown to more than 2,500.

Mr. Henry said FBI agents are increasingly coming across data stolen from companies whose executives had no idea their systems had been accessed.

"We have found their data in the middle of other investigations," he said. "They are shocked and, in many cases, they've

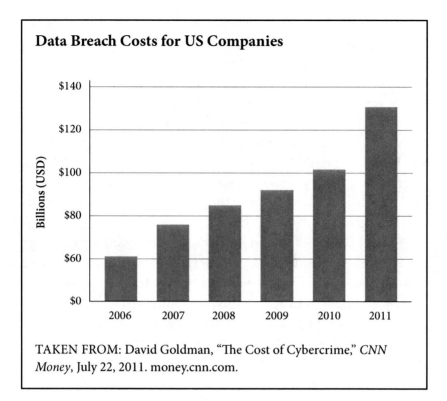

Data Breach Costs for US Companies

TAKEN FROM: David Goldman, "The Cost of Cybercrime," *CNN Money*, July 22, 2011. money.cnn.com.

been breached for many months, in some cases years, which means that an adversary had full visibility into everything occurring on that network, potentially."

Mr. Henry said that while many company executives recognize the severity of the problem, many others do not, and that has frustrated him. But even when companies build up their defenses, their systems are still penetrated, he said. "We've been playing defense for a long time . . . . You can only build a fence so high, and what we've found is that the offense outpaces the defense, and the offense is better than the defense," he said.

Testimony Monday before a government commission assessing Chinese computer capabilities underscored the dangers. Richard Bejtlich, chief security officer at Mandiant, a computer-security company, said that in cases handled by his firm where intrusions were traced back to Chinese hackers, 94% of the targeted companies didn't realize they had been breached until someone else told them. The median number of days between the start of an intrusion and its detection was 416, or more than a year, he added.

In one such incident in 2010, a group of Chinese hackers breached the computer defenses of the U.S. Chamber of Commerce, a major business lobbying group, and gained access to everything stored on its systems, including information about its three million members, according to several people familiar with the matter.

In the congressional debate over cybersecurity legislation, the Chamber of Commerce has argued for a voluntary, non-regulatory approach to cybersecurity that would encourage more cooperation and information-sharing between government and business.

Matthew Eggers, a senior director at the Chamber, said the group "is urging policy makers to change the 'status quo' by rallying our efforts around a targeted and effective information-sharing bill that would get the support of multiple stakeholders and come equipped with ample protections for the business community."

The FBI's Mr. Henry said there are some things companies need to change to create more secure computer networks. He said their most valuable data should be kept off the network altogether. He cited the recent case of a hack on an unidentified company in which he said 10 years worth of research and development, valued at more than $1 billion, was stolen by hackers.

He added that companies need to do more than just react to intrusions. "In many cases, the skills of the adversaries are so substantial that they just leap right over the fence, and you don't ever hear an alarm go off," he said. Companies "need to be hunting inside the perimeter of their network," he added.

Companies also need to get their entire leadership, from the chief executive to the general counsel to the chief financial officer, involved in developing a cybersecurity strategy, Mr. Henry said. "If leadership doesn't say, 'This is important, let's sit down and come up with a plan right now in our organization; let's have a strategy,' then it's never going to happen, and that is a frustrating thing for me," he said.

> "The multi-national, multi-jurisdictional nature of these cyber-crime cases has increased in complexity and, accordingly, increased the time and resources needed for successful investigation and adjudication."

A Multifaceted Strategy Is Best to Ensure Cybersecurity

Michael P. Merritt

Michael P. Merritt is the assistant director of the Office of Investigations for the US Secret Service. In the following viewpoint, he reports that federal authorities have observed a marked increase in the quality, quantity, and complexity of cybercrimes in the United States. Merritt argues that to effectively protect cybersecurity there needs to be a greater collaboration within the federal, state, and local law enforcement communities. He finds that a multifaceted approach to aggressively combat cyber and computer-related crime has worked effectively for the Secret Service and has resulted in the dismantling of some of the largest known transnational cyber-criminal organizations.

Michael P. Merritt, "Testimony Before the Senate Homeland Security and Governmental Affairs Committee," September 14, 2009.

As you read, consider the following questions:

1. According to Merritt, what is the Electronic Crimes Special Agent Program?
2. How many Electronic Crimes Task Forces have been established by the Secret Service, according to the viewpoint?
3. What does Merritt describe as the goal of the National Computer Forensics Institute?

In recent years, the Secret Service has observed a significant increase in the quality, quantity, and complexity of cyber-cases in which perpetrators target financial institutions in the United States. The combination of the information revolution and the effects of globalization have driven the evolution of the Secret Service's investigative mission. The advent of technology and the Internet created a new transnational "cyber-criminal," and as a result the Secret Service has observed a marked increase in cyber and computer-related crimes targeting private industry and other critical infrastructures. For example, trends show an increase in network intrusions, hacking attacks, malicious software, and account takeovers leading to significant data breaches affecting every sector of the American economy. As large companies have adopted more sophisticated protections against cyber-crime, criminals have adapted as well by increasing their attacks against small and medium-sized businesses, banks, and data processors. Unfortunately, many smaller businesses do not have the resources to adopt and continuously upgrade the sophisticated protections needed to safeguard data from being compromised.

Trends in Cyber and Computer-Related Crimes

The Secret Service is particularly concerned about cases involving network intrusions of businesses that result in the compromise of credit and debit card numbers and all related personal information. A considerable portion of this type of electronic theft appears to be attributable to organized cyber-groups, many of them based abroad, which pursue both the intrusions and the subsequent exploitation of the stolen data. Stolen credit card information is often trafficked in units that include more than just the card number and expiration date. These "full-info cards" include additional information, such as the card holder's full name and address, mother's maiden name, date of birth, Social Security number, a PIN, and other personal information that allows additional criminal exploitation of the affected individual.

Although network intrusions can be devastating to a company of any size, the subsequent theft of data and customer information often has more dire consequences on a small or medium-sized company that most likely does not have the resources or expertise necessary to properly protect their networks and data. For example, in October 2007, the Secret Service identified a complex fraud scheme in which servers owned by a payroll company were compromised by a network intrusion. Subsequently, four debit card accounts belonging to a small Midwestern bank were compromised, distributed online, and used in a coordinated attack resulting in ATM withdrawals in excess of $5 million. The withdrawals involved 9,000 worldwide transactions in less than two days and the bank had to file for Chapter 11 bankruptcy protection. Our investigation revealed that the criminals compromised the payroll company's database, reset PINs, loaded balances onto the accounts, and removed account withdrawal limits or set the limits at extremely high levels.

Through this investigation, the Secret Service also identified another organized cyber-group in New York City trafficking stolen credit card data that was transmitted by multiple suspects operating in Russia and the Ukraine. Following the investigative leads generated in this case, the Secret Service was able to prevent additional losses by notifying victims of the intrusion and compromise, often before the victims became aware of the illicit activity. For example, the Secret Service discovered that

"Hackers." © 2003 Arcadio Esquivel, Cagle Cartoons.

the computer network of a U.S. bank had been compromised. Subsequent notification by the Secret Service enabled the bank to significantly reduce its exposure and avoid potential losses exceeding $15 million. Based on these investigative efforts, the Secret Service identified 15 compromised financial institutions, $3 million in losses, 5,000 compromised accounts, and prevented more than $20 million in potential losses to U.S. financial institutions and consumers.

Cybercriminals Have Formed a Global Syndicate

The increasing level of collaboration among cyber-criminals raises both the complexity of investigating these cases and the level of potential harm to companies and individuals alike. Illicit Internet carding portals allow criminals to traffic stolen information in bulk quantities globally. These portals, or "carding websites," operate like online bazaars where criminals converge to trade in personal financial data and cyber-tools of the trade. The websites vary in size, from a few dozen members to some of the more popular sites boasting memberships of approximately 8,000 users. Within these portals, there are separate forums moderated by notorious members of the carding community. Members meet online and discuss specific topics of interest. Criminal purveyors buy, sell, and trade malicious software, spamming services, credit, debit, and ATM card data, personal identification data, bank account information, hacking services and other contraband.

Although increasingly difficult to accomplish, the Secret Service has managed to infiltrate many of the "carding websites." One such infiltration allowed the Secret Service to initiate and conduct a three-year investigation that led to the identification and high-profile indictment of 11 perpetrators involved in hacking nine major U.S. retailers and the theft and sale of more than 40 million credit and debit card numbers.

Conspirators Devise a Complex Scheme

The investigation revealed that defendants from the United States, Estonia, China, and Belarus successfully obtained credit and debit card numbers by hacking into the wireless computer networks of major retailers—including TJX Companies, BJ's Wholesale Club, OfficeMax, Boston Market, Barnes & Noble, Sports Authority, and Dave & Buster's. Once inside the networks, they installed "sniffer" programs that would capture card numbers, as well as password and account information, as they moved through the retailers' credit and debit processing networks.

After they collected the data, the conspirators concealed the data in encrypted computer servers that they controlled in the United States and Eastern Europe. They then sold some of the credit and debit card numbers via online transactions to other criminals in the United States and Eastern Europe. The stolen numbers were "cashed out" by encoding card numbers on the magnetic strips of blank cards. The defendants then used these cards to withdraw tens of thousands of dollars at a time from ATMs. The defendants were able to conceal and launder their fraud proceeds by using anonymous Internet-based electronic currencies within the United States and abroad, and by channeling funds through bank accounts in Eastern Europe.

The total actual loss associated with this investigation is still being assessed. However, one of the corporate victims has already reported expenses of almost $200 million resulting from the intrusion.

In both of these cases, the ripple effects of the criminal acts extend well beyond the company compromised. In one example alone, millions of individual card holders were affected. Although swift investigation, arrest, and prosecution prevented many consumers from direct financial harm, all of the potential victims were at risk for misuse of their credit cards, overall identity theft, or both. Also, costs suffered by businesses, such as the need for enhanced security measures, reputational damage, and direct financial losses, are ultimately passed on to consumers.

Fighting Cybercrime Requires Collaboration

While cyber-criminals operate in a world without borders, the law enforcement community does not. The multi-national, multi-jurisdictional nature of these cyber-crime cases has increased in complexity and, accordingly, increased the time and resources needed for successful investigation and adjudication. For example, in the TJX investigation, the Secret Service not only worked with domestic law enforcement partners, but also with officials from Thailand, the United Arab Emirates, Turkey, Ukraine, Spain, Belarus, Estonia, and Germany. The complexity of this three-year investigation involved personnel from our San Diego, Miami, and Boston Field Offices working in close coordination with personnel from our Headquarters Divisions.

Recognizing these complexities, several federal agencies are collaborating to investigate cases and identify proactive strategies. Greater collaboration within the federal, state, and local law enforcement community enhances information sharing, promotes efficiency in investigations, and facilitates efforts to de-conflict in cases of concurrent jurisdiction. As a part of these efforts and to ensure that information is shared in a timely and effective manner, the Secret Service has personnel detailed to the following DHS [Department of Homeland Security] and non-DHS entities:

- National Protection and Program Directorate's (NPPD)— Office of the Under Secretary;
- NPPD's National Cyber Security Division (US-CERT);
- NPPD's Office of Infrastructure Protection;
- Department of Homeland Security's Science and Technology Directorate (S&T);
- White House Homeland Security Staff;
- Department of Justice National Cyber Investigative Joint Task Force (NCIJTF);
- Each Federal Bureau of Investigation Joint Terrorism Task Force (JTTF), including the National JTTF;
- Department of the Treasury—Terrorist Finance and Financial Crimes Section
- Department of the Treasury—Financial Crimes Enforcement Network (FinCEN);
- Central Intelligence Agency [CIA];
- National Security Council [NSC];
- The Drug Enforcement Administration's International Organized Crime and Intelligence Operations Center;
- Europol [European Police Office]; and
- INTERPOL [International Criminal Police Organization]

To continue to fulfill our obligation to protect our financial infrastructure, industry, and the American public, the Secret Service has adopted a multi-faceted approach to aggressively combat cyber and computer-related crimes. The Secret Service has dismantled and continues to dismantle some of the largest known transnational cyber-criminal organizations by:

- providing the necessary computer-based training to enhance the investigative skills of special agents through our Electronic Crimes Special Agent Program (ECSAP);
- collaborating with other law enforcement agencies, private industry, and academia through our 28 Electronic Crimes Task Forces (ECTF);
- identifying and locating international cyber-criminals involved in network intrusions, identity theft, credit card fraud, bank fraud, and other computer-related crimes through the analysis provided by our Criminal Intelligence Section (CIS);
- providing state and local law enforcement partners with the necessary computer-based training, tools, and equipment to enhance their investigative skills through the National Computer Forensics Institute (NCFI);
- maximizing partnerships with international law enforcement counterparts through our international field offices; and
- maximizing technical support, research and development, and public outreach through the Secret Service CERT Liaison Program (CLP) at Carnegie Mellon University.

A Look at the Electronic Crimes Special Agent Program

A central component of the Secret Service's cyber-crime investigations is its Electronic Crimes Special Agent Program (ECSAP). This program is comprised of 1,148 Secret Service special agents who have received at least one of three levels of computer crimes-related training. These agents are deployed in more than 98 Secret Service offices throughout the world and have received extensive training in forensic identification, preservation and retrieval of electronically-stored evidence. ECSAP agents are computer investigative specialists and among the most highly-trained experts in law enforcement, qualified to conduct examinations on all types of electronic evidence. This core cadre of special agents is equipped to investigate the continually evolving arena of electronic crimes and have proven invaluable in the successful prosecution of criminal groups involved in computer fraud, bank fraud, identity theft, access device fraud, and various other electronic crimes targeting our financial institutions and private sector.

The ECSAP program is divided into three levels of training and focus:

Level I—Basic Investigation of Computers and Electronic Crimes (BICEP). The BICEP training program focuses on the investigation of electronic crimes and provides a brief overview of several aspects involved with electronic crimes investigations. This program is designed to provide Secret Service agents and our state and local law enforcement partners with a basic understanding of computers and electronic crime investigations. The BICEP program has proven so effective that the Secret Service has incorporated it into its core curriculum for newly hired special agents.

Currently, the Secret Service has 823 special agents trained at the BICEP level.

Level II—Network Intrusion Responder (ECSAP-NI). ECSAP-NI training provides special agents with specialized training and equipment that allows them to respond to and investigate network intrusions. These may include intrusions into financial sector computer systems, corporate storage servers, or various other targeted platforms. The Level II trained agent will be able to identify critical artifacts that will allow effective investigation of identity theft, malicious hacking, unauthorized access, and various other related electronic crimes.

Currently, the Secret Service has 161 special agents trained at the ECSAP-NI level.

Level III—Computer Forensics (ECSAP-CF). ECSAP-CF training provides special agents with specialized training and equipment that allows them to investigate and forensically obtain legally admissible digital evidence. The forensically obtained digital evidence is utilized in the prosecution of various electronic crimes cases, as well as criminally focused protective intelligence cases.

Currently, the Secret Service has 164 special agents trained at the ECSAP-CF level.

The Role of Electronic Crimes Task Forces

In 1996, the Secret Service established the New York Electronic Crimes Task Force (ECTF) to combine the resources of academia, the private sector, and local, state, and federal law enforcement agencies to combat computer-based threats to our financial payment systems and critical infrastructures. Congress has since directed the Secret Service in Public Law 107-56 to establish a nationwide network of ECTFs to "prevent, detect, and investigate various forms of electronic crimes, including potential terrorist attacks against critical infrastructure and financial payment systems."

The Secret Service has established 28 ECTFs, including the first international ECTF based in Rome, Italy. Membership in our ECTFs include: 299 academic partners; over 2,100 international, federal, state, and local law enforcement partners; and over 3,100 private sector partners. The Secret Service ECTF model is unique in that it is an international network with the capabilities to focus on regional issues. For example, the New York ECTF, based in the nation's largest banking center, focuses heavily on protecting our financial institutions and infrastructure, while the Houston ECTF works closely with partners such as ExxonMobil, Chevron, Shell, and Marathon Oil to protect the vital energy sector. By joining our ECTFs, all of our partners enjoy the resources, information, expertise, and advanced research provided by our international network of members while focusing on issues with significant regional impact.

Criminal Intelligence Section Supports International Investigations

Our Criminal Intelligence Section (CIS) collects, analyzes, and disseminates data in support of Secret Service investigations nationwide and overseas and generates new investigative leads based upon its findings. CIS leverages technology and information obtained through private partnerships to monitor developing technologies and trends in the financial payments industry for information that may be used to enhance the Secret Service's capabilities to prevent and mitigate attacks against the financial and critical infrastructures.

CIS has developed an operational unit that investigates international cyber-criminals involved in cyber-intrusions, identity theft, credit card fraud, bank fraud, and other computer-related crimes. The information and coordination provided by CIS is a crucial element to successfully investigating, prosecuting, and dismantling international criminal organizations.

National Computer Forensics Institute Offers Critical Training

The National Computer Forensics Institute (NCFI) initiative is the result of a partnership between the Secret Service, the Department of Homeland Security (DHS), and the State of Alabama. The goal of this facility is to provide a national standard of training for a variety of electronic crimes investigations. The program offers state and local law enforcement officers, prosecutors, and judges the training necessary to conduct computer forensics examinations. Investigators are trained to respond to network intrusion incidents and conduct basic electronic crimes investigations.

Since opening on May 19, 2008, the Secret Service [NCFI initiative] has provided critical training to 564 state and local law enforcement officials representing over 300 agencies from 49 states and two U.S. territories.

Collaboration of International Partners

One of the main obstacles that agents investigating transnational crimes encounter are jurisdictional limitations. The Secret Service believes that, to fundamentally address this issue, appropriate levels of liaison and partnerships must be established with our foreign law enforcement counterparts. Currently, the Secret Service operates 22 offices abroad, each of which has regional responsibilities providing global coverage. The personal relationships that have been established in those countries are often the crucial element to the successful investigation and prosecution of suspects abroad.

Computer Emergency Response Team Provides Research and Support

In August 2000, the Secret Service and Carnegie Mellon University Software Engineering Institute (SEI) established the Secret Service CERT Liaison Program (CLP). The role of the CLP is threefold: (1) technical support; (2) research and development; and (3) public outreach and education.

The CLP is a collaborative effort with over 150 scientists and researchers engaged in the fields of computer and network security, malware analysis, forensic development, and training and education. Supplementing this effort is research into emerging technologies being employed by cyber-criminals, and development of technologies and techniques to combat them.

The objectives of the CLP are: to broaden the Secret Service's knowledge of software engineering and networked systems security; to expand and strengthen Secret Service partnerships and relationships with the technical and academic communities; to provide an opportunity for the Secret Service to work closely with CERT, SEI, and Carnegie Mellon University; and to provide public outreach and education.

Examining the Heartland Payment Systems Case

As an example, the partnerships developed through our ECTFs, the support provided by our Criminal Intelligence Section, the liaison established by our overseas offices, and the training provided by ECSAP were all instrumental to the Secret Service's successful investigation into the network intrusion of Heartland Payment Systems (HPS). An August 2009 indictment alleges that a transnational organized criminal group used various network intrusion techniques to breach security, navigate the credit card processing environment, and plant a "sniffer" to capture payment transaction data.

The Secret Service investigation revealed data from more than 130 million credit card accounts at risk of being compromised and ex-filtrated to a command and control server operated by an international group directly related to other ongoing Secret Service investigations. During the course of the investigation, the Secret Service uncovered that this international group committed other intrusions into multiple corporate networks to steal credit and debit card data. The Secret Service relied on various investigative methods, including search warrants, the use of Mutual Legal Assistance Treaties with our foreign law enforcement partners, and subpoenas to identify three main suspects. As a result of this investigation, the three suspects in the case were indicted and charged with various computer-related crimes.

This case represents the largest and most complex data breach investigation ever prosecuted in the United States.

Fighting Cybercrime Requires Innovation

Today, hundreds of companies specialize in data mining, data warehousing, and information brokerage. This wealth of available personal information creates a target-rich environment for today's sophisticated criminals. However, businesses can provide a first line of defense by safeguarding the information they collect. Such efforts can significantly limit the opportunities for these criminal organizations. Furthermore, the prompt reporting of major data breaches involving sensitive personally identifiable information to the proper authorities will help ensure a thorough investigation is conducted. The Secret Service and DHS continue to collaborate closely with the private sector to improve coordination and communication on cyber issues.

As I have highlighted here, the Secret Service has implemented a number of initiatives on cyber and computer-related crimes. Responding to the growth in these types of crimes and the level of sophistication these criminals employ demands an increasing amount of resources and greater collaboration. Accordingly, we dedicate significant resources to increasing awareness, educating the public, providing training for law enforcement partners, and improving investigative techniques. The Secret Service is committed to our mission of safeguarding the nation's critical infrastructure and financial payment systems. We will continue to aggressively investigate cyber and computer-related crime to protect consumers.

In conclusion, I would like to reiterate that cyber-crime remains an evolving threat. It is not a threat of the future; it is very much here. Law enforcement agencies must be able to adapt to emerging technologies and criminal methods. The Secret Service is fully involved in the federal government's new approach to cybersecurity. We are dedicated to the government's collective effort to adopt innovation in our approach to cyber-crime and cybersecurity and to stay ahead of this ever-changing threat. The Secret Service is pleased that the Committee recognizes the magnitude of these issues and the constantly changing nature of these crimes; to effectively fight this crime, our criminal statutes must be amended to safeguard sensitive personally identifiable information and to afford law enforcement the appropriate resources to investigate data breaches.

> *"Even the strongest proponents of cybersecurity legislation acknowledge that the private sector will take a leadership role in protecting America's online infrastructure."*

Private Sector Isn't Waiting for Feds to Deal with Internet Security

John Hayward

John Hayward is a staff writer at Human Events. *In the following viewpoint, he maintains that private industry is taking a leadership role in fighting cybercrime and protecting US computer networks from hackers. The US government, Hayward asserts, needs to let private industry take the lead without imposing burdensome regulations that would impede security strategies or add massive costs. Hayward argues that the private sector is motivated to take on this momentous challenge because they are keen to defend their businesses from cyberthreats.*

As you read, consider the following questions:

1. According to Larry Clinton, how much did the private sector spend on cybersecurity in 2011?

2. What is the global value of the security software market, according to the market research firm Canalys?

3. What does the Ponemon Institute estimate is the current average level of safety from online attack?

Congressional efforts to introduce cybersecurity legislation have failed this summer, at least for the time being, but the private sector has hardly been idle in creating defenses against hackers and viral threats.

Some details of this security activity must necessarily be kept secret, because cyber-war defenders cannot afford to tip their hand to hackers. Online security is analogous to a military intelligence operation at every level, from vendors providing antiviral solutions for home users, to massive corporate security structures.

This makes it difficult to put together a broad picture of private security efforts, but Larry Clinton, president of the Internet Security Alliance, estimated before a House Energy and Commerce subcommittee in February that private sector security spending totaled an astonishing $80 billion in 2011.

This expense covers a constantly evolving defensive architecture, which must cope with eternally mutating viral threats and innovative hacking techniques. Most personal users can get a faint impression of how quickly this game of cat-and-mouse plays out by noting how frequently their personal anti-virus software is updated.

Multiply that sense of urgency by a billion, and you have an idea of the challenge faced by top-level Internet security experts.

Nothing to Sneeze At

Those little personal-computer antivirus programs are nothing to sneeze at. A huge amount of work goes into designing and updating them. Top security software companies, such as Symantec and McAfee, publish enormous databases of viral threats, which

The Dynamism of Private Industry

Even as the U.S. government strengthens its cadre of cyber-security professionals, it must recognize that long-term trends in human capital do not bode well. The United States has only 4.5 percent of the world's population, and over the next 20 years, many countries, including China and India, will train more highly proficient computer scientists than will the United States. The United States will lose its advantage in cyberspace if that advantage is predicated on simply amassing trained cybersecurity professionals. The U.S. government, therefore, must confront the cyberdefense challenge as it confronts other military challenges: with a focus not on numbers but on superior technology and productivity. High-speed sensors, advanced analytics, and automated systems will be needed to buttress the trained cybersecurity professionals in the U.S. military. And such tools will be available only if the U.S. commercial information technology sector remains the world's leader. . . .

Making use of the private sector's innovative capacity will also require dramatic improvements in the government's procedures for acquiring information technology. On average, it takes the Pentagon 81 months to make a new computer system operational after it is first funded. Taking into the account the growth of computing power suggested by Moore's law, this means that by the time systems are delivered, they are already at least four generations behind the state of the art. By comparison, the iPhone was developed in 24 months. That is less time than it would take the Pentagon to prepare a budget and receive congressional approval for it.

William J. Lynn III, "Defending a New Domain," US Department of Defense, 2010.

they update daily. McAfee offers visitors to its website a global virus map, and a viral threat level indicator similar to the one used by the Department of Homeland Security for terrorist threats. Symantec has a global risk timeline, which graphically tracks the detection and defeat of viral threats from day to day.

Market research firm Canalys projects that 2012 will see a nearly 9 percent increase in sales of security software, bringing the global value of that market to $22.9 billion. Heated competition from many different vendors for a share of that immense market has kept the cost of security software for home users remarkably low. In fact, programs from some vendors can be downloaded for free, while even the more powerful and highly regarded packages for home users cost about the same as a video game.

And yet, some observers believe that even this enormous private-sector investment in security is not sufficient. A study prepared by Bloomberg News, in cooperation with a research firm called the Ponemon Institute, concluded that a core group of industries and government agencies would need to boost security spending by nearly 800 percent to achieve 95 percent protection against electronic attack.

Financial companies were said to require a 1,300 percent increase in spending to achieve such a level of safety. The Ponemon Institute estimated that the current average level of safety from online attack is only about 69 percent.

Interestingly, respondents to this study had to be promised anonymity to participate, because it is so risky to discuss the details of cybersecurity programs.

Storm-tossed Electronic Ocean

This, of course, led to calls for government to compel the necessary increases in security spending, through some combinations of incentives and mandates. Part of the problem is that computer systems have become tightly connected through the Internet. A high-security system exposes itself to danger by allowing connections from a lower-security system. This leads high-security system operators to desire minimum standards of integrity for every system they interact with.

That was much easier to arrange when "online" connections involved modems dialing into carefully protected phone numbers. Now that online interconnectivity is a real-time, always-on sea of high-speed communications, security threats are greatly magnified. Nearly every computer device has a theoretical connection to every other device.

Yesterday's critical systems were fortresses with occasional leaks in their data plumbing; now they're tiny boats forever adrift in a storm-tossed electronic ocean. And we have yet to witness the Internet equivalent of a hurricane sweeping across that sea of data: an orchestrated cyber-attack launched by a hostile foreign power.

One of the greatest concerns facing private-sector security operations is the question of legal liability. Legislators want private teams to coordinate with each other, and the government, to detect and defeat large-scale online threats. Private corporations worry this could get them sued by angry users for violating their privacy.

The value of the data at risk from electronic sabotage is difficult to determine, and no corporate manager relishes the thought of conducting that evaluation before a jury, with millions of dollars in damages on the line. It's difficult to determine what a reasonable investment in defense measures should be, when the value of the digital property at risk cannot be readily calculated.

Another serious problem facing private security teams is the danger of making their defenses so tough that legitimate users find it difficult to access their systems, compromising the value of the products and services they offer. There's an old saying in the computer world that 100 percent security can be achieved only by unplugging your computer. No profitable electronic enterprise wants to risk "unplugging" itself from the Internet, by implementing security procedures its customers find excessively inconvenient.

Even the strongest proponents of cybersecurity legislation acknowledge that the private sector will take a leadership role in protecting America's online infrastructure. The challenge is to achieve the right level of information sharing and data security without imposing ruinous costs on private enterprises, or compromising the flexibility of the fast-moving online security industry by submerging it beneath a bureaucratic quagmire.

Business managers are keenly interested in defending their operations from serious threats, but less enthusiastic about spending massive sums to buy protection from hypothetical menaces. On the Internet, hypothesis can become practical reality with astonishing speed.

> *"Ethical hacking sounds like an oxymoron, but it's essential to cybersecurity."*

Ethical Hacking Improves Cybersecurity

Sue Marquette Poremba

Sue Marquette Poremba is a contributor to SecurityNewsDaily. In the following viewpoint, she promotes the benefits of ethical hacking—a practice that tests corporate cybersecurity in order to better identify weaknesses and improve computer systems. Poremba argues that such rigorous investigations are key to addressing the challenge of cybersecurity. It is thought, she maintains, that the skills possessed by ethical hackers are valuable and should be promoted in today's advanced technological age.

As you read, consider the following questions:

1. What is another term for ethical hackers, according to Poremba?
2. What does Poremba list as common backgrounds for ethical hackers?
3. What does Poremba perceive to be the most important benefit of utilizing ethical hackers?

When you think of hackers and hacking, do you picture groups like Anonymous launching high-profile attacks that target email passwords and personal information?

Or do you see high-school kids in their bedrooms, logging into school networks to change their grades? We usually think hacking and hackers are bad. Sometimes, that's true. But hacking can also be done for the greater good, and that's where "ethical hacking" comes in.

Ethical hacking sounds like an oxymoron, but it's essential to cybersecurity.

Testing the Boundaries

"Ethical hacking is the practice and exercise of testing a company's security measures and business practices in an effort to identify vulnerabilities and weaknesses that threaten their assets," said Luke McOmie, director of Lambda Labs at Red Lambda, a data-security-software provider based in Longwood, Fla. "The purpose of this testing is to produce information that judges the company's security posture against industry/international security standards."

Ethical hackers use the same tools and techniques that malicious hackers use to penetrate a network or deceive humans in order to identify weaknesses in technology and employees, said Renee Chronister, an ethical hacker with Parameter Security in St. Peters, Mo.

Ethical hackers, also known as penetration testers or "pen testers," see how far they can get into a company or organization's network and what sensitive data they can access. They use this information not to their advantage, but to the company's advantage, so that it can better lock down its network.

Ethical Hackers Are Perpetual Problem Solvers

Most ethical hackers are professionals who may have started off hacking computers many years ago and developed skills over time. Some have systems- and network-administrator backgrounds. Others are former software developers. Some have mathematical backgrounds, while others have scientific training.

"Regardless of the background, truly effective ethical hackers love a challenging puzzle," said Ed Skoudis, a SANS Institute Faculty Fellow and founder of Counter Hack Challenges, an educational organization devoted to information security. "They revel in taking things apart to find their flaws."

"Some ethical hackers focus on security research, discovering flaws in products, protocols and new technologies," Skoudis said. "Penetration testers focus on finding flaws in organizations' deployed systems."

"Penetration testing, in essence, is the application of ethical hacking skills and techniques to a specific deployed technical infrastructure," he said. "Some ethical hackers are security researchers and penetration testers."

Ethical Hackers Provide Insight

Perhaps most importantly, ethical hackers provide valuable insight into how an attacker thinks, how he or she will form an attack and what the attacker's next move will be.

"Because of this, we can fix holes before they become targets," said Charles Tendell, a "certified ethical hacker" based in Denver.

That's how ethical hackers promote better cybersecurity.

"If you don't know where your security holes are, then how can you protect against malicious attacks?" Chronister said. "Ethical hacking identifies and exploits your weaknesses so you can see what sensitive data can be assessed and empowers you by being able to remediate these weaknesses hopefully before malicious hackers strike."

To become an ethical hacker, Skoudis said, one should spend time learning how computer systems and networks really work. A deep view and understanding of technology is vital to finding flaws and manipulating systems.

Skoudis believes hacking is a skill that everyone should have.

"One of the things I do with my kids is hold periodic 'Skoudis Family Hacking Nights,'" he said. "When I tell some of the folks in my neighborhood about this, they look at me in horror. I then explain to these folks that hacking can be done for noble purposes, with a focus on helping improve the state of security."

As technology becomes a more important part of most people's lives, Skoudis added, the ability to find flaws in it and to manipulate it is increasingly valuable for people in all walks of life.

> *"I'm also not saying that you shouldn't hire a hacker, just don't make them out to be something that they're not."*

Exploding the Myth of the "Ethical Hacker"

Conrad Constantine and Dominique Karg

Conrad Constantine is a research engineer, and Dominique Karg is chief hacking officer at Alien Vault, an online-security management company. In the following viewpoint, they consider the idea of an "ethical" hacker, finding the term to be contradictory. Constantine and Karg contend that a hacker finds a way to clandestinely infiltrate complex, protected security systems, and that being a hacker is a mindset involving breaking the rules. Therefore, the authors argue, even an ethical hacker is still a hacker.

As you read, consider the following questions:

1. What do the authors identify as two connotations associated with the term "hackers"?
2. What argument do the authors say would not be an adequate defense for people charged with hacking?

3. According to the authors, what makes a hacker desirable as an employee?

The subject of whether or not to hire an "ethical hacker" has been debated since the 90s, albeit with perhaps a little less misdirection back then. We'd argue that the "ethical" hacker simply does not exist, so perhaps the time has come for a new question, about whether we should even use the term "ethical hacker."

If you find yourself on the wrong side of a locked door, you do not think to yourself "I need an ethical locksmith"—unless you're a thief, in which case you probably have a whole host of other questions. Instead, you look for a locksmith, pure and simple. You trust that the person that turns up to break your lock will do no more, and no less, than the job you've hired him for. Calling him ethical does not legitimize his practice of breaking in.

So why is there a need to justify hiring a hacker by claiming he's "ethical?" In my opinion, the job title itself is the problem.

An Ethical Hacker Is Still a Hacker

The term "hacker" has two connotations:

- someone that has been convicted of a computer related criminal activity, or
- someone who thinks a certain way about technology.

If you consider it a term that refers to criminal intentions then you're basically saying "ethical criminal." How is it possible to argue that that makes sense when it's obviously a contradiction?

On the other hand, if you are using it to describe a person who thinks about technology in a certain way, then why does it need the word "ethical" in front of it?

Redefining Hacking

This takes us back to our ethical locksmith argument.

Yes, hackers have had bad press for many years, but calling the practice "ethical" will not change that. The job of the hacker is to clandestinely look for ways to infiltrate systems. What is then done with that access is the differentiator.

It's easy right now to pick on bankers who are having a hard time, especially as many are being tarred fraudsters and thieves. However, we don't see any of these professionals clamouring to repackage themselves as "ethical" to distance themselves from their unsavory peers.

Examining the Hacker Mindset

Some hackers would argue that they're not criminals, but activists. Others would say that they're just rebellious in the way they think about technology and have a duty to highlight an organisation's poor security. Does that make them unethical?

We need people who are willing to stand up and challenge authority—in so doing, does that then make them ethical? We don't see why it should.

It just means that they can look at something—an application or a business process, for example—and can see why something won't work and are willing to explain why—or better still how it can be improved.

A case in point is the Fukushima nuclear disaster. A report into the incident stated that the disaster was completely preventable. It wasn't the earthquake, or resulting tsunami, that was to blame but human error, or human oversight, spawned from a culture of unquestioning obedience. All it would have taken was for one person to stand up and state that the various technical processes employed to implement safety regulations, rather than preventing an accident, could fail.

And that's precisely a hacker's mindset—not to take things for granted, to question authority and challenge the regimented way of doing something that pushes back on the status quo. Ethical or unethical doesn't come into the equation.

Hiring a "Non-Criminal"

We would concede that for many convicted of hacking it could be argued that there are extenuating circumstances.

For example, a few years ago it was almost impossible to get access to code to learn on your own, resulting in many resourceful technical people being convicted of "hacking." Today, this argument of "I had to hack so I could learn" would not be considered adequate defence as the availability of virtual infrastructure technologies—among other interesting tools—means there is so much more that can be set up in your own home to learn your craft.

Additionally, Germany's "Hacking" law defines many security tools as illegal purely because of their design and ability. For that reason, you don't even have to be doing anything with these tools that could harm someone to be found guilty of hacking.

This ambiguity has resulted in the argument that not all hackers are criminals and therefore the term "ethical" started to be used. While we would agree that not all hackers are criminals, we would therefore also argue that the term "ethical" is unnecessary.

Ultimately it comes down to the fact that most organizations would not hire a criminal—therefore why do we need "ethical" in front of hacker to prove this.

Moving on from the last argument, it doesn't seem logical to refer to someone as an "ethical hacker" because he or she has moved over from the dark side "into the light." It just makes them a bad hacker. Kevin Mitnick isn't famous because of his skills—he's famous because he got caught.

And before we move on from talking about skills, we'd like to clarify that "ethical hacking certificates" aren't worth the paper they're printed on. The reason you want to employ a hacker is not because they know the "rules" to hacking, can run them and produce reports. What makes a hacker desirable as an employee is the very fact that they don't play by the rules, with an "anything that works" mentality, as it's this combination that will give them the skills to test your systems to the very limit.

Who Is Kevin Mitnick?

A convicted felon who is now a security expert, Kevin Mitnick has written two books illustrating how personal and corporate computer security can be breached. As a teenage hacker and "phone phreak," Mitnick and his friends searched dumpsters for computer information. His first arrest came when he was just seventeen and hacked into Pacific Bell's computers in 1981. Mitnick went on to become one of the most notorious computer con men in the United States. When he was convicted for stealing long-distance codes from MCI in 1989, his defense included the claim that he was "addicted" to computers. After serving a year in federal prison, he was required to complete a residential twelve-step program. In 1992 federal officials sought Mitnick in another Pacific Bell case, which caused him to go into hiding for more than two years. He was discovered in North Carolina after he broke into the home computer of computational physicist Tsutomu Shimomura. Arrested in early 1995, he was charged with forty-eight counts of computer, wire, and cell-phone fraud. It was not until 1999, though, that Mitnick pleaded guilty to seven charges, having served most of a five-year sentence.

Mitnick asserts that his interest in hacking was never about causing harm; rather, he got a thrill out of accomplishing the seemingly impossible and impressing others. After three years' probation, he was allowed back on the Internet and founded his own consulting company. He is now in the business of teaching others how he used "social engineering" to gain access to sensitive information.

"Kevin Mitnick," Contemporary Authors
Online, *2012.*

Don't Legitimize Hacking

When people use the term "ethical" hacker, they mean someone who is good at breaking into things by using creative techniques and methods but without the criminal intention. However, my case is that the inclusion of the term "ethical" does not legitimize the practice. It is still hacking—end of argument.

I'm also not saying that you shouldn't hire a hacker, just don't make them out to be something that they're not. If they're a hacker—they're a hacker. By describing them as ethical does not necessarily make them ethical, or unethical for that matter.

And for hackers, you have a talent and should not have to hide it under a rock because some people practice the art for malicious or fraudulent reasons.

If we're too embarrassed to openly admit that we need and want a hacker to test our systems then let's give them a new name not legitimize the practice. Answers on a postcard please.

Periodical and Internet Sources Bibliography

The following articles have been selected to supplement the diverse views presented in this chapter.

Robert B. Dix	"Congress Can't Improve Cybersecurity Alone," *Politico*, August 21, 2012. www.politico.com.
Joseph Menn	"Hacked Companies Fight Back with Controversial Steps," *Reuters*, June 17, 2012. www.reuters.com.
Evgeny Morozov	"What Fearmongers Get Wrong About Cyberwarfare," *Slate*, May 28, 2012. www.slate.com.
Craig A. Newman and Daniel L. Stein	"A Need for Clearer Disclosure Rules After Cyberattacks," *New York Times*, November 9, 2012. www.nytimes.com.
Amy Payne	"Morning Bell: Do You Trust the Government with Your Computer?," *The Foundry*, November 14, 2012. blog.heritage.org.
Pamela Ryckman	"Owners May Not Be Covered When Hackers Wipe Out a Business Bank Account," *New York Times*, June 13, 2012. www.nytimes.com.
Bernard Scaglione	"How to Fight Back Against Hackers," *Security Magazine*, October 1, 2012. www.securitymagazine.com.
Loren Thompson	"Five Things the Government's Cybersecurity Providers Should Have—and Usually Don't," *Forbes.com*, June 18, 2012. www.forbes.com.
John Villasenor	"Why the Government Can't Remain the Cybersecurity Czar," *Brookings Institute*, May 3, 2012. www.brookings.edu.
Samuel Visner	"The Risky Business of US Government Cyber Security," *Forbes.com*, April 30, 2012. www.forbes.com.

OPPOSING
VIEWPOINTS®
SERIES

Is Hacktivism a Serious Threat?

Chapter Preface

In the wake of the Arab Spring—a series of pro-democracy protests that started in Tunisia in 2010 and subsequently swept through the Middle East and North Africa—the country of Syria has been roiled by devastating violence and instability. The initial protests in Syria began in early 2011 as anti-government rallies against the harsh rule of President Bashar al-Assad. They culminated in nationwide demonstrations and demands for the resignation of Assad as well as the end of secular rule by the dominant Ba'ath Party. Many of these demonstrations erupted into violence between the protestors and local security forces. At first, Assad tried to placate the protestors with promises of significant democratic reforms. When the protests continued, the violence escalated into an all-out civil war.

The Syrian Civil War has been waged on several fronts. There has been the conventional battle between protestors and government forces fighting on the streets, resulting in tragic deaths and horrible injuries in cities and villages across the country. There has been a diplomatic conflict, as the global diplomatic community pressures the Syrian government to ease its military response and search for a peaceful solution. Sectarian battles have erupted, as long-simmering tensions between various religious sects have escalated into violence within Syria. There has also been a cyberwar raging between hacktivists supporting the Syrian rebel forces and the Syrian Electronic Army, an organized group of hackers launching attacks on Facebook, Twitter, and other websites in support of the Syrian government.

Hacktivism is a term that refers to hacking in support of a political or social movement. Early in the Syrian Civil War, hacktivists worked to publicize the government crackdown and human rights violations perpetrated by the Assad regime. They posted citizen videos of protests, violence, and wanton brutality by local security forces online and created campaigns on Facebook and Twitter that provided eyewitness testimonies and pictures from protestors on the ground as events unfolded. Such campaigns not only raised awareness of the events in Syria but also inspired political support for international efforts to address the violence. Hacktivism proved instrumental in bringing the Syrian Civil War to the forefront of international diplomatic efforts and keeping the pressure on the United Nations to militarily intervene in the ongoing conflict.

In response, hackers who support the Assad government began a campaign of their own to disrupt anti-government websites and put out a competing narrative about the war. In 2012, these hacktivists, who call themselves the Syrian Electronic Army, managed to launch three types of cyberattacks: defacement of Syrian opposition websites; defacement of Western websites; and spamming popular Facebook pages. In some of their most successful actions, they were able to hack the Facebook pages of a number of world-famous figures, including US President Barack Obama and TV talk show host Oprah Winfrey to post pro-Assad messages. They also managed a coordinated attack on the US Department of Treasury website and the legendary hacking collective known as Anonymous.

These pro-Assad hacktivists have no official connection to the Syrian government. On June 20, 2012, however, Assad acknowledged their efforts, stating that "young people have an important role to play at this stage, because they have proven themselves to be an active power. There is the Electronic Army which has been a real army in virtual reality."

The role of hacktivism in political and social movements is discussed in the following chapter. Authors examine hacktivism as a threat to civil liberties, free speech, and national security and a tool for positive social, economic, and political change.

| "I believe that yes, hacktivism is a
genuine form of protest."

Hacktivism Is an Effective and Ethical Means of Social Protest

Graham Armstrong

Graham Armstrong is a contributor to ORG Zine, *an online magazine of the Open Rights Group, a digital rights organization. In the following viewpoint, he finds that hacktivism is an ethical form of social protest. It is an effective way to protest, he says, because it has the potential to generate publicity and sympathy for important causes. However, he argues that its serious nature requires it to be one of the final options of protest for use when all other methods of protest have failed. Hacktivism can intimidate and alienate potential supporters as easily as it can challenge and engage them, Armstrong concludes.*

As you read, consider the following questions:

1. According to the author, hacktivism is a combination of what two common words?
2. Who is The Jester, according to Armstrong?
3. How does Armstrong define the term "dox drops"?

In the online age of uncertain digital rights, it's crucial for individuals to take a stand and raise awareness of the issues that affect all of us online. There's several ways within the online world to demonstrate and raise awareness of causes such as e-petitions or social networking groups, but one of the more controversial methods is *hacktivism*. The term *hacktivism* is a portmanteau of the words *hacker* and *activist* which tends to refer to the use of unauthorised computer access to further an agenda, usually political or social. Hacktivism itself can be a fairly dubious issue, for all the power it can grant hackers of varying shades of grey, it could potentially be an effective tool for promoting an important agenda.

Scrutinizing the Effectiveness of Hacktivism

It's very difficult for activists in small numbers to bring awareness to the issues that they campaign against. It's tempting for activists to pull stunts in order to raise awareness of their cause; take the instance of Eddie Gorecki and Jonathan Stanesby, two members of Fathers 4 Justice, who scaled the Royal Courts of Justice dressed as Batman and Robin. Their protest managed to gain national recognition in the press, which rather successfully raised their profile. Days later two-thousand supporters marched in London *with a tank!*

So perhaps hacktivism is just that—the gimmick that raises the profile of a cause. Anonymous hacktivists have used the Low Orbit Ion Cannon (LOIC), a tool for Distributed Denial of Service (DDoS) attacks, to take down several websites of organisations supporting the Stop Online Piracy Act. The Department of Justice website was taken down as well as those owned by the FBI, MPAA [Motion Picture Association of America, and] RIAA [Recording Industry Association of America]. Was it effective? Well SOPA [Stop Online Piracy Act] failed, didn't it?

That said, I wouldn't attribute the success of the anti-SOPA campaign to Anonymous taking down websites. At most, I could imagine people trying to access those sites being irritated that "their internet isn't working properly." Many of the examples of hacktivism I've seen are preaching to the converted; this style of hacktivism does not seem to do much to engage with the public beyond creating momentary annoyances.

I believe that most of the attention to the anti-SOPA campaign came from the blackout of prominent websites such as Wikipedia, Reddit and Craigslist. This seemed a brilliant strategy to confront end-users with the effects of censorship, perhaps more-so than a "500 Internal Error" web page.

However, aside from black-outs, there is also the case of internet vigilantes such as "The Jester" who put a lot of effort into disrupting the websites of alleged terrorist organisations. As of late, he's also helped to put behind bars several "script-kiddies" who disrupted the UK anti-terrorist hotline as well as disrupt the activities of Anonymous group LulzSec. If there's such a thing as hacktivism in action—that's it!

Is Hacktivism Ethical?

On the face of it, a lot of DDoS attacks can seem to simply be retaliation—an eye for an eye. I've never been comfortable with that stance. To me, activism should be about rectification rather than revenge. So can hacktivism ethically meet this criteria?

It could be seen that hacktivism in the form of website take-downs and take-overs is a method of censorship. Denying access to information from groups with opposing viewpoints could be seen as dodgy behaviour, however I'm not ready to brand this as censorship. I feel that censorship is a very strong term describing the suppression of ideas; this sort of website blocking is more comparable to graffiti than book burning. These actions often take websites offline for a few hours, nothing serious enough to cause lasting damage but just enough to raise attention to a cause. Consider as well that this behaviour could be a form of disobedience in refusing to accept services as-is; that perhaps attacks like these are comparable to blockading buildings like the

Online Piracy and SOPA

The popularity of foreign-based websites that allow users to download or share copyrighted media skyrocketed in the second decade of the twenty-first century. The number of visitors to peer-to-peer sites such as Pirate Bay has more than doubled since the beginning of 2010, with more than one billion monthly page views as of late 2011. Although some of the media is in the public domain, much of it is protected under U.S. copyright law, which ensures compensation to the owners of such media, including music, video, and eBooks. Estimates of the economic impact of online piracy vary widely, but almost everyone agrees that the music and film industries have lost revenue and jobs over the past decade due to the increasingly popular practice of illegal file sharing.

As a result of these concerns, the United States Congress has attempted several times to create more stringent laws to protect intellectual property. The latest measures, proposed in 2011, included a bill by the U.S. Senate, the Protect Intellectual Property Act (PIPA), and another bill by the U.S. House of Representatives, the Stop Online Piracy Act (SOPA), authored by Texas Congressman Lamar Smith. Although both bills sought to block access to non–U.S.-based sites accused of piracy, SOPA went further than PIPA in mandating that search engines such as Google remove any links to these sites.

"Online Piracy and SOPA," Global Issues in Context Online Collection, *2012.*

recent protest in Mexico against biased TV reporting or even the Occupy movement.

It's easy enough to imagine however that the owners of these websites won't see having their own content effectively blocked as a legitimate act of protest. It'd be all too easy for groups of organised hackers to pick on somebody whose livelihood depends on their web presence. It's unlikely to be that bad; targets of hacktivist attacks tend to be large multi-national corporations like Visa, to whom a few angry nerds with a DDoS script pose little risk. But the key question as to whether these attacks are justified does not have a blanket answer; it will always depend on the specific case.

A tactic that certainly should be of concern to digital rights campaigners is *document dropping* or as it's referred to: "dox drops." This is the practise of hackers stealing personal, or otherwise private, information pertaining to individuals and publishing it to the web. Personal details of executives of the pro-copyright lobby were published to the world as part of Anonymous' *Operation Payback*. Clearly that was a breach of individual privacy and served no purpose for pursuing an agenda, other than an incitement of retaliation.

I feel this comes down to an argument of "does the ends justify the means?" If we consider that using hacktivist methods could disrupt terrorist networks or promote a particular cause or ideology, are we willing to accept that it's ok? At the end of the day, hacktivists have to accept that it's as important for those they disagree with to share their opinion as it is for those they oppose.

Hacktivism Should Be the Last Resort

I've spent a while thinking about this but I believe that yes, hacktivism *is* a genuine form of protest. Clearly from the attention that has been given to causes utilising hacktivist methods it seems fair to say that hacktivism can be effective. I find it debatable though as to whether hacktivist methods can create sympathy for a cause; it's difficult to ascertain the helpfulness of hacktivism for a particular cause. I do believe that it is entirely possible for hacktivist methods to be used in a justified and ethical way.

The serious nature of hacktivism necessitates that it be one of the final options of protest for when all other methods have failed. It's a rather aggressive tactic that's more likely to intimidate and aggravate rather than promote progressive discourse between two parties. Failing that, clever clogs hackers will no doubt find a way to promote their message.

> "Slowly, popular culture is perverting the image of the Internet criminal, transforming him or her into a noble figure of free speech, dissent and speaking truth to power."

Hacktivist Collectives Are Terrorists

Phil Elmore

Phil Elmore is a freelance writer and contributor to WorldNetDaily, *an online news site. In the following viewpoint, he contends that US national security is under a cyberattack launched by a range of enemies, from China to WikiLeaks to unnamed hackers bent on destroying US infrastructure. Hacker collectives like WikiLeaks, he asserts, are particularly dangerous because they are romanticized by those on the political Left, who call them "hacktivists" and praise them as crusaders for free speech. Elmore argues that they are really terrorists and those who excuse their actions are terrorist sympathizers.*

As you read, consider the following questions:

1. Who does Elmore identify as the founder of WikiLeaks?
2. According to Elmore, how did National Public Radio describe hacker attacks?

3. What Left-leaning celebrity does Elmore blame for romanticizing hacktivism as practiced by WikiLeaks?

In last week's Technocracy [a blog on the *WorldNet Daily* website], I wrote about the WikiLeaks controversy. More specifically, I wrote about the ways intimidation of a website owner's support and infrastructure services—services paid for by the website in question—can silence or impede the expression of free speech. I made no real attempt to evaluate the activities of WikiLeaks or its founder, Julian Assange, except to say that I consider Mr. Assange little better than a terrorist. Most of Mr. Assange's difficulties have, to this point, revolved around issues that were anything *but* an evaluation of whether he has committed a crime.

Cyberwarriors Are Attacking US Infrastructure

Recent news has made it easier to characterize WikiLeaks and Assange politically and socially. It has also underscored, starkly, the real war we fight in contemporary society. We fight this war regardless of our knowledge of it. We win or lose this war despite the widespread ignorance of it that often characterizes our governments, our allies and our citizenry.

In the summer of 2009, I first wrote of this war in "Why we need cyber-warriors now." In that column, I spoke of a "proxy war" even now "taking place behind the veil of modern technology." I will repeat now what I said then: Every minute of the day, external foes are mounting assaults on American infrastructure, civilian American assets and American military targets. Those enemies do this through the virtual world. Their foot soldiers are an army of disparate computer hackers, ranging from state-sponsored operatives to ordinary people in almost every nation on the planet.

The problems don't stop with the hostile governments of emerging military and technological threats like China. According to Popsci.com, it isn't just China's government that is attacking our cyber-infrastructure. It's also hundreds of thousands of Chinese civilians. . . . The FBI can do little to prosecute hackers in foreign countries, least of all hostile nations like China (whose government turns a blind eye to simple copyright infringements, much less wholesale cyber war). The hackers are also becoming harder to monitor and track through conventional means.

Hacktivism Is a Myth

The problem is that "hackers" are no longer "hackers." Slowly, popular culture is perverting the image of the Internet criminal, transforming him or her into a noble figure of free speech, dissent and speaking truth to power. This imagery is fiction, if for no other reason than it is not now, nor has it ever been, a noble act of freedom of expression to harass, silence or harm commercially an entity whose lawful activity you dislike. Yet this is precisely what has happened—and "hackers" are now "hacktivists," presumed by wretched propagandists like Michael Moore to be committing acts of "patriotism" rather than propagating wanton electronic vandalism, fraud, intimidation and theft.

Many Americans first became aware of "hacktivism" last week [December 2010], when supporters of WikiLeaks, angered by several commercial firms' withdrawal of services to Assange and his organization, targeted these businesses for denial-of-service attacks (and other electronic crimes). Media outlets were quick to declare that "the first global cyber war has begun," characterizing these criminal acts in sickeningly fawning articles as acts of resistance against "authoritarian regimes" and "obvious symbols of authority." National Public Radio called the hack-attacks "surprisingly easy social protest," while columnist Chris O'Brien said these virtual terrorist attacks signal a "rise of new powers," a potentially "epic" erosion of national sovereignty that redefines how we describe and affiliate ourselves as citizens.

The wide-eyed adoration of criminals and agitators by left-wing pundits and "journalists" around the world should not

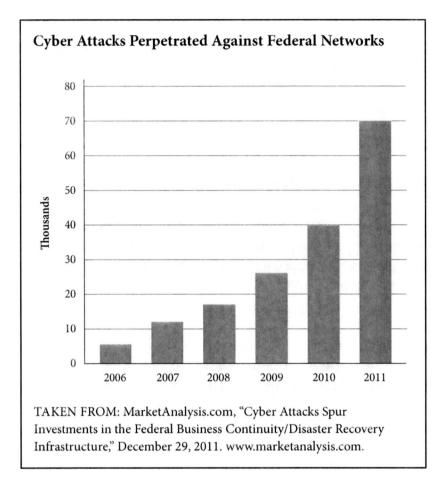

Cyber Attacks Perpetrated Against Federal Networks

TAKEN FROM: MarketAnalysis.com, "Cyber Attacks Spur Investments in the Federal Business Continuity/Disaster Recovery Infrastructure," December 29, 2011. www.marketanalysis.com.

surprise us. Such left-wing socio-political functionaries adore anything that repudiates American exceptionalism or otherwise diminishes American power and influence. This is why, predictably, a host of left-leaning public figures—Michael Moore included—are so quick to hold up Assange as some kind of crusader for free speech . . . rather than the simple agent of espionage he is by *definition*. A man who releases confidential information to a worldwide information network, regardless of how he came by that information, is simply *disseminating classified information obtained illegally*. Such a man is free to do so if he truly wishes to go to war with the nation(s) whose documents he is publicly sharing, but he should not then whine that as an icon of free expression, he should be free of the far-reaching consequences for his actions.

Hacktivism Is a National Security Threat

In judging the nature of Assange and WikiLeaks, we must come back to "hacktivism." When hackers distribute a computer virus to disable Iran's nuclear program, they are arguably acting in the best interests of all concerned. When hackers crash the websites of Visa, Mastercard or PayPal because they're mad that these organizations won't funnel money to Assange and his terrorist organization, they're simply bullies. The difference is not a question of whose side you happen to be on, much as leftists would have us believe. The difference is found in the context of these acts. Right and wrong exist. Rogue nations with nuclear weapons are a threat to peaceful citizens around the world. Banking firms that refuse to finance Julian Assange's releases of confidential documents aren't hurting or threatening anyone; they have the choice to refuse commerce they find objectionable or disreputable.

You may say that it is unfair to judge Assange and his organization by the criminal acts of their supporters. WikiLeaks does not control the actions of supposedly anonymous hackers or the hateful bloviating of cretins like Michael Moore, you may point out. You would be right, too. Assange, however, told us everything we need to know about him by creating and distributing an encrypted "doomsday" file, the key to which will be released if Assange judges he has been sufficiently misused by those in power. What is this if not extortion—and what is extortion if not the tool, the fundamental source of power, of a terrorist?

Julian Assange is a terrorist. We know this by his actions. His supporters are those who hate and fear America. By *their* words and deeds, we know them to be terrorist sympathizers.

"Libertarian distrust of government, belief in networks of free citizens, mistrust of copyright and intellectual property laws, and a drive for self-determination appear to unite the hacktivist fringe."

Hacktivists Fight for Civil Liberties and Free Expression

James Ball

James Ball is a reporter for The Guardian. *In the following viewpoint, he reports that the main motivating factors of hacktivist collectives are to fight government efforts at cybersurveillance, protect the open nature of the Internet from government regulation and censorship, and hold public authorities to account. Ball explores the implications of these hacker principles and the attempts of governments to limit the ability of hacktivists to fulfill their goals. These attempts have become more aggressive, he explains, and the battles over the future of the Internet have become more political in nature. In response, Ball relates, hacktivists have begun to organize and wield some political muscle to protect themselves and their principles.*

As you read, consider the following questions:

1. According to Ball, what US senator called on companies to cut WikiLeaks?
2. Where was the Pirate Party founded, according to the viewpoint?
3. How many Bitcoins are there in existence, according to Ball?

If there is a battle over the future shape of the internet—and society as a whole—then hacktivist groups such as Anonymous and Lulzsec, Wikileaks and the file-sharing site Megaupload.com are among the frontline battalions.

While the individual incidents and clashes involving these groups may seem disparate and unconnected, those at the core of online activism say all these organisations, plus relatively mainstream movements such as Occupy and the Pirate Party, are linked.

The Goal of Hacktivists

John Perry Barlow, lyricist for the Grateful Dead and co-founder of the well-known advocacy group Electronic Frontiers Foundation (EFF), says the over-arching motivation of such efforts, whatever tactics are used, was to shift the nature of society.

"What unites these groups is the belief that the future is not about vertical, hierarchical government, but horizontal [peer-to-peer] government," he said. "This pits the forces of the information age against those of the industrial age, as we move from scarcity of information to abundance. The last year has established our ability to have revolutions, but not to govern in their wake—but that's coming.

"Different groups are on a spectrum. Organisations like the EFF would be on the conservative end. Along the way is WikiLeaks and the Pirate party, with Anonymous at the more radical end."

Though ties between the groups are often tenuous, a broadly shared ideology of a libertarian distrust of government, belief in networks of free citizens, mistrust of copyright and intellectual property laws, and a drive for self-determination appear to unite the hacktivist fringe of the internet.

Political Hackers Are the Enemy of the State

Barlow believes the US government has started aggressively pursuing political hackers such as Anonymous and Lulzsec. The groups mounted attacks taking US and UK government websites offline, targeted News International, allegedly taking a tranche of emails belong to staff of the Sun, and took the full email archives of US intelligence firm Stratfor and passed them to WikiLeaks.

"The government targets Anonymous for the same reason it targets al-Qaida—because they're the enemy. And in a way, they are. The shit is starting to hit the fan, but we haven't started to see the effects of that yet. The internet is the most liberating tool for humanity ever invented, and also the best for surveillance. It's not one or the other. It's both."

Barlow is working on a system to oppose the financial blockade imposed against WikiLeaks. In the wake of WikiLeaks' publication of US diplomatic cables, Senator Joe Lieberman called on US companies to cut off the site. Payment providers Visa, Mastercard and Paypal acceded to the request, despite no order or request coming from government, starving the site of funding.

Protecting Free Speech on the Internet

Barlow is planning the establishment of a foundation aimed at funding any organisations affected by corporate blockades with first amendment implications.

"We hope it makes a moral argument against these sorts of actions," he says. "But it could also be the basis of a legal challenge. We now have private organisations with the ability to stifle free expression. These companies have no bill of rights that applies to their action—they only have terms of service."

As a result, battles over the future of the internet are becoming increasingly politicised as opposing sides try to set the legal framework. A huge network of grassroots organisations coalesced in the US to fight the stop online piracy act (Sopa). The bill was eventually stopped in its tracks as opposition mounted, but similar efforts in the EU and elsewhere have had more success proceeding through the legislature.

Hacktivists Are Getting Political

On other fronts, cyber-surveillance is increasing, with the UK government proposing a law to allow the monitoring of information on emails, social network and Skype traffic on all users in real-time. To fight such efforts, hacktivists are getting political.

The best known movement of this sort is the Pirate party, which was founded in Sweden by Rickard Falkvinge in 2006 and is marginal in the UK but is building up substantial influence across the world. The party has two MEPs [Member of European Parliament] in the European parliament, and recently took 7.4% of the vote in recent elections in the Saarland region of Germany—and according to recent polls it is now the third biggest in the country.

The party has even briefly had a cabinet minister, Slim Amamou, a Tunisian activist who served as sports and youth minister in his country for a brief period last year before resigning in protest over web censorship imposed by Tunisia's army.

Amelia Andersdotter, one of the party's two MEPs, thinks authorities tend to ignore the political element of hacking attacks by groups such as Anonymous.

"Some of these hacking attacks are misconstrued. Many are clearly politically targeted, attempts to register protest at something a government or organisation is doing," she says. "There is a lack of understanding in cyber-security. Things are seen as big and intimidating when they are often not.

"Suddenly, denial of service attacks [an attack that floods a site with fake traffic and prevents people from visiting] which used to be legal in many member states, are being prosecuted. Most of these used to be for bad reasons, attacks by rivals, but now more than half are political and there are more prosecutions."

Andersdotter's priorities are looking into how public authorities' security efforts are regulated and held to account, attempting to reform the EU's intellectual property laws, and helping to spread fibre internet—faster broadband speeds—across the EU.

Opening the Internet

Others aren't content merely to lobby politicians for a free internet. Instead, they have built tools designed to make regulating the internet an impossible task. One of the most widely used is Tor, short for "the onion router".

Tor, when used properly, anonymises all internet traffic coming from a machine by bouncing it around dozens of other computers around the world, taking a different path each time. This means an individual will only be identifiable when he or she chooses to log into a given site.

The system is not infallible, as it can be blocked—temporarily—by authoritarian governments, but provides a huge degree of protection, whether to activists working in oppressive regimes, or to those using the internet to smuggle drugs or share child pornography.

The Benefits of Open Internet

This dilemma has not gone unnoticed by the people behind the tools.

"Criminals will always be opportunists and will see new prospects before everyone else does," says the Tor project's executive director, Andrew Lewman. "Old-fashioned police work still works incredibly well against such people. Almost every transaction in the UK uses EFT [card payment], there is CCTV on every street, and monitoring of online communications—but you still have trafficking and other crimes.

"The benefits of the open internet work much the same as motorways or interstates: they outweigh the costs. In the US, police opposed the building of interstate roads, saying they would help criminals circumvent the law. But the police adapted, and the benefits of highways clearly outweigh the costs."

Lewman says the main motivating factor behind the Tor project is not to overthrow government, or even to engage in activism, but rather to give users control over how they use the internet and who is able to monitor their activity. But he is not surprised that governments are trying to regulate the internet.

"Governments are stalling to realise a growing share of their GDP depends on the internet. Government like stability, not rapidly shifting ground," he concludes.

But government could be circumvented entirely, as coders haven't only been building ways of circumventing legal oversight: they have built a whole new stateless currency from the ground up.

The Power of an Internet Currency

The currency is known as Bitcoin, and relies on a series of mathematical algorithms to govern the amount of money in circulation and the future inflation rate. Each Bitcoin has a unique ID and transactions are recorded in public ledgers, making fraud far more difficult than most real-world currencies—but as Bitcoins aren't backed by a government, if they're stolen, they're gone forever, as some early adopters found out to their cost.

At the time of writing, there are more than 8.7m Bitcoins in existence, worth a total of around $42.3m (£26.2m). The combination of a stateless currency and untraceable internet use is a powerful one, as one underground site highlights.

The Silk Road is a website only accessible in the "dark" section of Tor, meaning it can't be viewed or traced on the general

The Pirate Party

The Pirate Party wants to fundamentally reform copyright law, get rid of the patent system, and ensure that citizens' rights to privacy are respected. With this agenda, and only this, we are making a bid for representation in the European and Swedish parliaments. Not only do we think these are worthwhile goals. We also believe they are realistically achievable on a European basis. The sentiments that led to the formation of the Pirate Party in Sweden are present throughout Europe. There are already similar political initiatives under way in several other member states. Together, we will be able to set a new course for a Europe that is currently heading in a very dangerous direction.

"The Pirate Party," www.piratpartiet.se,
2012.

internet, and accepts only Bitcoins for payment. The site allows the buying and selling of illegal drugs, predominantly in the US, UK and Netherlands.

Its existence isn't a secret. In 2011 two senators wrote to the US attorney general asking for action to be taken against the site, which was described as a "one-stop shop for illegal drugs that represents the most brazen attempt to peddle drugs online that we have ever seen".

Action against the site, which operates in a similar manner to eBay, linking independent buyers and sellers, has so far proved impossible, and the publicity generated for the Silk Road only boosted its—and Bitcoin's—popularity.

Promoting such enterprises is not, though, the driving motivation for most of the people behind the development of Bitcoin.

The Goals of Bitcoin

One core member of Bitcoin's development team, Amir Taaki, explains the broad motivations of the hacktivist movement from a "hackspace" in east London—a loose members' club designed to let people build, code and tinker as they wish. Even the space's door is customised: it's tailored to open when members pass their Oyster card or similar radio-frequency ID nearby, and then plays a customised greeting (one has chosen the victory theme from Final Fantasy VII, a cult 90s videogame).

The first principle of hacker culture, Taaki says that "all authority should be questioned". He stresses this doesn't mean governments or police are necessarily corrupt, or aren't needed, but that the public should always be in a position to hold such authorities to account.

This leads to the second core principle: information should, generally speaking, be free. Copyright laws, patents, government secrecy and more are a huge target for the movement.

The Implication of Hacker Principles

What this would mean for industries such as pharmaceuticals, where a pill may cost pennies to make but millions to research is unclear, though—and Taaki doesn't have the answers. What he does raise is a challenge. To date, it's the entertainment industries—Hollywood, music, television and publishers—that have felt the effects of piracy and filesharing. Developments in technology mean that may not remain the case for long.

Devices known as 3D printers are able to create real-life objects based on three-dimensional plans. The technology is expensive: a cheap commercial machine costs upwards of £10,000, but a build-it-yourself open source version has already been conceived. The RepRap can be built for just over £300. Intriguingly, a RepRap can currently produce around half the parts needed to make another one. Given enough time, the devices will likely be able to print out the parts to make a whole new 3D printer—a self-replicating machine.

It's a technology with impressive potential, the ability to "print" virtually any item that can be conceived—tools, toys, even food—but the applications to date are fairly basic, and costly. At present, the printers can mainly make novelty items—though early, successful attempts to clone plastic Warhammer toys led to lawsuits and a predictable backlash.

A technology that could allow anyone to manufacture any item, given the right blueprints, heralds a huge storm for any company relying on old-world business models—and today's hackers know it.

"The battle between pirates and the music or film industries is really nothing, it's a warm-up," Taaki says. "When this technology matures, manufacturers, agriculture businesses, technology firms, any of this could be easily replicated by almost anyone, anywhere. That's when we'll see the real fight—and they don't even see it coming."

> *"Hacktivism is a civic ethic that I think is integral to a liberal democratic society today, but with one caveat. I don't condone breaking the law."*

Old-Time Hacktivists: Anonymous, You've Crossed the Line

Elinor Mills

Elinor Mills is a reporter for CNET News. *In the following viewpoint, she finds that several pioneers of the hacktivism movement are opposed to the methods of the new generation, who disable information and data networks as acts of political activism. These early hacktivists, she explains, deem the new methods to be counterproductive and a violation of Internet freedom. One of the goals of hacktivism, Mills points out, is the protection of free speech and the free expression of ideas on the Internet; website defacement, data theft, and distributed denial-of-service attacks are antithetical to those ideals.*

As you read, consider the following questions:

1. According to Mills, who coined the term "hacktivist"?
2. What was Operation Iran, according to the author?

3. What group does Mills identify as the one that popularized the notion of distributed denial-of-service attacks for political protest?

In December 1998, a U.S.-based hacker group called Legions of the Underground declared cyberwar on Iraq and China and prepared to protest human rights abuses in those countries by disrupting their Internet access.

About a week later, a coalition of hackers from groups including Cult of the Dead Cow (cDc), L0pht, Chaos Computer Club in Germany, and hacker mags 2600 and Phrack issued a statement condemning the move. "We—the undersigned—strongly oppose any attempt to use the power of hacking to threaten to destroy the information infrastructure of a country, for any reason," the statement said. "One cannot legitimately hope to improve a nation's free access to information by working to disable its data networks."

Legions of the Underground got the message and backed down. The hackers went back to embarrassing Microsoft by exploiting security weaknesses in Windows, partying at Def-Con in Las Vegas, and testing the line between white hat and gray hat security as they explored the limits and frontiers of technology.

But the line that was drawn back then is again being crossed.

This time it's hackers and online activists working under the banner of Anonymous who are using Web site defacements, distributed denial-of-service (DDoS) attacks, and data theft, ostensibly to press their campaign for Internet freedom and human rights. The group, because of its lack of leadership and organization, also finds itself calling for seemingly contradictory operations including both urging people to vote in the elections this year as part of Occupy the Vote [a political movement] and a "declaration of war" on the U.S. over proposed cybersecurity legislation, urging a vague destruction of the government but not a computer attack or physical protest.

The former "chief evangelist for hacktivism" at the cDc, Oxblood Ruffin, says this is not the way of a true hacktivist.

"Anonymous is fighting for free speech on the Internet, but it's hard to support that when you're DoS-ing and not allowing people to talk. How is that consistent?" Oxblood Ruffin said in an interview this week with CNET. "They remind me of awkward teenagers. I think they're trying to do the right thing, but they're stumbling around and doing some really stupid sh**."

Hacktivismo

The cDc members were early hacktivists. A member named Omega coined the term "hacktivist" in an e-mail to the group in 1996, partly tongue-in-cheek. "We were providing ridicule and social commentary," Oxblood Ruffin said. "We were opinion leaders in the computer underground."

A fun quip turned into much more, though, starting with the Hong Kong Blondes. This was a mysterious group of Chinese dissidents with handles like Lemon Li and Databyte Cowgirl, who apparently were being advised by the cDc and other hackers in the use of encryption to circumvent China's Great Firewall. In an interview with Oxblood Ruffin in July 1998 leader Blondie Wong announced the formation of a new international group called the Yellow Pages that he said would hack into the computer networks of U.S. corporations doing business with China. (Some people have questioned the veracity of the colorful stories from Wong, who claimed to be an astrophysicist. Oxblood Ruffin declined to disclose much more about the group, but promised further revelations in the future.)

In 1999 the cDc created an offshoot group called "Hacktivismo" that included hackers, lawyers and activists. The hackers developed, contributed to and distributed tools designed to help dissidents in repressive regimes avoid censorship and surveillance. Those wares included: Peekabooty, which allowed people to bypass national firewalls; Camera/Shy, a steganography application that allowed people to hide content within other content;

secure instant messaging client software ScatterChat; and Tor, which allows people to use the Internet anonymously.

The Hacktivismo Declaration was released in 2001 and it stated that "full respect for human rights and fundamental freedoms includes the liberty of fair and reasonable access to information, whether by shortwave radio, air mail, simple telephony, the global Internet, or other media." In addition, "state sponsored censorship of the Internet erodes peaceful and civilized coexistence, affects the exercise of democracy, and endangers the socioeconomic development of nations," it proclaimed.

Later, in a paper entitled "Hacktivism, From Here to There" that Oxblood Ruffin presented at the CyberCrime and Digital Law Enforcement Conference at Yale Law School in March 2004, hacktivism is defined as "using technology to improve human rights across electronic media." And he laid down some ground rules—no DDoS attacks and no Web site defacements.

"In my opinion and in the UN Declaration on Human Rights access to information, access to speech, access to privacy are all guaranteed human rights," Oxblood Ruffin said this week. "So, you either believe in free speech, or you don't. You either believe in privacy, or you don't."

"Things like DDoSing, defacements, data theft, in broad strokes I don't subscribe to at all in liberal democracies. I don't agree with their tactics when they involve those things, but like many people I share their broader concerns," he said, referring to Anonymous' criticism of corporate control over the U.S. political and financial system, as well as support for the Arab Spring and uprisings in countries like Egypt, Tunisia, Libya, Syria, and elsewhere.

"When you abridge speech, when you abridge the First Amendment, people have died protecting these rights and all of a sudden we have a vigilante group deciding who can speak, and they are deciding who can access that speech," he added.

However, Oxblood Ruffin praised one operation that involved shutting down a Web site—Operation Iran, in which hackers took down Web sites the regime was using to publish hit lists of protesters' photos for government supporters to target. "If you are saving life, then I don't have an issue with data theft or DDoS," he said.

He also said he strongly supports the use of social media such as Twitter and YouTube to promote human rights, a technique Anonymous has certainly mastered to positive effect. "That's a classic example of hacktivism," he said of Anonymous helping protesters organize and get around attempts at government censorship.

Electronic Disturbance Theater

Another long-time online political activist disagrees with the Oxblood Ruffin's criticism of Anonymous. Ricardo Dominguez, a co-founder of The Electronic Disturbance Theater (EDT) and associate professor of new media arts at the University of California in San Diego, said there are times when defacements and DDoS attacks are appropriate acts of electronic civil disobedience.

"The history of civil disobedience, with Gandhi, Martin Luther King Jr. and Henry David Thoreau, is one of blockage or trespass . . . that disrupts the everyday flow of power," Dominguez said in an interview. "As a community, do we value information to such a degree that brief moments of disturbance" can not be tolerated even though they are designed for protest and to help right moral wrongs?

Formed by Dominguez and other artists and researchers in 1997, the EDT popularized the notion of DDoS for political protest and created FloodNet, one of the first tools designed to flood Web sites with so much traffic that they were temporarily crippled. They called their DDoS attacks "virtual sit-ins" and used the tool against Mexican government sites in solidarity with the Zapatista rebels in Chiapas, Mexico.

More recently, the group released the Transborder Immigrant Tool, which is a Motorola i455 cell phone with a Global

Positioning System app that is designed to help people crossing the U.S.-Mexico border figure out their location and find water caches left by activists.

While Anonymous participants are anonymous out of necessity to avoid prosecution, the EDT members were committed to "radical transparency" and their online and offline personas were exposed, Dominguez said. But he can see why Anonymous hides behind their Guy Fawkes masks.

"The EDT understands there are political, government, and corporate spaces where one can not be transparent," he said. "Where any form of political protest, no matter how non-violent, will always be met with direct violence in some way."

Like the EDT, there is an offline component to Anonymous. Supporters have taken to the streets in protests against the Church of Scientology as part of Project Chanology in 2008 and in Occupy Wall Street demonstrations around the country last year. "I think Anonymous has been very effective, both as a network and as the emergence of a type of civil society and one that is extremely intimate with Net culture," Dominguez said.

Anonymous has also beefed up the firing power of its DDoS attacks compared with the early FloodNet tool, making such attacks easier to accomplish with automation. And Anonymous has been effective at recruiting supporters to lend their computers to the fire power.

"A Qualitative Difference"

It is this greater scale and anonymity of Anonymous operations that troubles Ron Deibert, who as director of The Citizen Lab at the Munk School of Global Affairs at the University of Toronto has been studying hacktivism for over a decade.

"With a physical sit-in, people are putting their lives on the line standing in front of a building. It's limited in scope and requires a physical commitment," he said. "Today, anyone with a $200 laptop can bring about a blockage, essentially silence a Web site into oblivion. There is no real physical risk to that, so it can be kind of frivolous. I think there's a qualitative difference between the two because of that."

There are times when it is acceptable to break the law, and those who participate in civil disobedience accept the risks, he said. "Whereas, online the ease with which anybody can create havoc and silence speech is much greater."

Deibert worries that stretching the definition of civil disobedience in this manner is prompting police and prosecutors to make criminals out of youngsters who don't understand the consequences of their actions. And he is concerned that the movement will ultimately lead to greater authoritarian control over the Internet and a diminishment of freedoms.

"I fear when the other shoe is going to drop," he said. "Among those of us who care about a free and open Internet, our attention needs to be focused on how we can restrain that type of behavior. When Anonymous attacks they play right into the hands of those who want to re-engineer the Internet because of security concerns."

Deibert agrees with the basic premise of Oxblood Ruffin's complaint, that shutting down Web sites of opponents is not viable protest.

"Impingement on free speech is not an appropriate form of political action in a democratic society," he said. "Hacktivism is a civic ethic that I think is integral to a liberal democratic society today, but with one caveat. I don't condone breaking the law."

Periodical and Internet Sources Bibliography

The following articles have been selected to supplement the diverse views presented in this chapter.

Idan Aharoni	"Hacktivism: Where It's Been and Where It's Going," *Security Week*, May 30, 2012. www.securityweek.com.
Dominic Basulto	"Does Hacktivism Mean the End of Ideology?," *Washington Post*, April 20, 2012. www.washingtonpost.com.
Brian Bennett	"Civilian 'Hacktivists' Fight Terrorists Online," *Los Angeles Times*, September 8, 2012. www.latimes.com.
Misha Glenny	"Tap into the Gifted Young Hackers," *New York Times*, March 8, 2012. www.nytimes.com.
David Goldman	"Lulzsec and Anonymous Are the Least of Your Hacker Worries," CNN.com, July 25, 2011. www.cnn.com.
Dan Kaplan	"Can Anonymous Force Its Victims to Reconsider Their Actions?," *SC Magazine*, January 31, 2012. www.scmagazine.com.
Oliver Rochford	"The Evolution of the Hacktivist Threat," *Security Week*, May 17, 2012. www.securityweek.com.
Jim Romeo	"Hacktivism Endures," *SC Magazine*, March 1, 2012. www.scmagazine.com.
Somini Sengupta	"The Soul of the New Hacktivist," *New York Times*, March 17, 2012. www.nytimes.com.
Eric Sterner	"Hacktivists' Evolution Changes Cyber Security Threat Environment," *World Politics Review*, April 23, 2012. www.worldpoliticsreview.com.

 CHAPTER 3

What Is the Significance of WikiLeaks?

Chapter Preface

The debate over WikiLeaks has illuminated a much larger debate over national security, government transparency, the implications of free speech on the Internet, and the role of media in today's ever-evolving technological age. Officially launched in 2007, the WikiLeaks website was initially established with the intention of providing transparency and sparking debate about oppressive regimes in many parts of the world, particularly Asia, Africa, the Middle East, and Eastern Europe. It published secret information provided by whistleblowers, including emails, reports, diplomatic cables, texts, and video that revealed unethical corporate practices, military activities, and government programs. According to WikiLeaks' website:

> Our goal is to bring important news and information to the public. We provide an innovative, secure and anonymous way for sources to leak information to our journalists (our electronic drop box). One of our most important activities is to publish original source material alongside our news stories so readers and historians alike can see evidence of the truth.

The head of the WikiLeaks organization is Julian Assange, an Australian publisher, journalist, and activist. Other early members included mathematicians, intelligence analysts, cryptographers, computer engineers, and activists. Most members of the organization choose to remain anonymous in light of the controversial nature of WikiLeaks' work. A nonprofit organization that relies on public donations, WikiLeaks has published thousands of documents and videos provided by anonymous whistleblowers that have sparked governmental and journalistic investigations as well as criminal prosecutions.

WikiLeaks first attracted international attention in December 2006 when it published a document signed by Somali political leader Sheikh Hassan Dahir Aweys that called for the assassination of multiple Somali government officials. The staff of WikiLeaks couldn't confirm the document's authenticity, but they published it with a disclaimer.

On November 7, 2007, WikiLeaks posted a copy of the Camp Delta Standard Operating Procedures, a document that detailed the administrative procedures used at Guantanamo Bay, a controversial US detention camp in Cuba used to hold high-value terrorist suspects. The document showed that US officials deliberately kept prisoners off-limits to the International Committee of the Red Cross, which the United States had repeatedly denied.

In another highly-publicized case, WikiLeaks released a classified video taken from an Apache helicopter showing the killing of ten Iraqi citizens and two Reuters journalists in April 2010. Known as the "Collateral Murder" video, it garnered international attention and led to various interpretations of what was actually on the video. From Assange's perspective, the video showed the cold-blooded murder of Iraqi citizens and two journalists; from the US military's view, it was a justifiable attack on suspected terrorist targets.

Cablegate is regarded as one of WikiLeaks' most extensive and controversial cases. On November 28, 2010, WikiLeaks began releasing scores of classified US diplomatic cables through agreements made with five major newspapers: the *New York Times*; *The Guardian* in Britain; *Der Spiegel* in Germany; *Le Monde* in France; and *El País* in Spain. The cables—confidential text communications between personnel at US embassies abroad and the US Department of State or other agencies—revealed a range of sensitive information. The WikiLeaks website maintains that:

> The cables show the extent of US spying on its allies and the UN; turning a blind eye to corruption and human rights abuse in "client states"; backroom deals with supposedly neutral countries; lobbying for US corporations; and the measures US diplomats take to advance those who have access to them. This document release reveals the contradictions between the US's

public persona and what it says behind closed doors—and shows that if citizens in a democracy want their governments to reflect their wishes, they should ask to see what's going on behind the scenes.

The revelations in the Cablegate documents were reported in newspapers around the world and embarrassed the US government, especially the US Department of State. It had far-reaching implications for ongoing diplomatic efforts, political initiatives and partnerships, and US foreign relations.

The significance of WikiLeaks is explored in the following chapter. The viewpoints discuss WikiLeaks as a threat to national security, the public's desire for transparency and accountability from its government, and the impact of WikiLeaks on free speech.

> "You can complain about some of the
> editorial decisions that WikiLeaks'
> managers have made, but as with the
> free press in general, we're better off
> with the site than without it."

WikiLeaks Provides Transparency and Can Deter Corporate and Government Misbehavior

Jesse Walker

Jesse Walker is an author and the managing editor of Reason. *In the following viewpoint, he commends the openness and transparency provided by WikiLeaks, a hacktivist collective that he maintains has provided invaluable information on covert government activities and corruption around the world. Walker argues that the world is better off when powerful, hierarchal institutions know that they are being monitored and that their illegal activities will be revealed by courageous whistleblowers. With more transparency comes accountability, he concludes, and government and corporations may act with more integrity if they know journalists, grassroot activists, and human rights campaigners are keeping track of their actions.*

As you read, consider the following questions:

1. Who does Walker identify as the US soldier who allegedly leaked classified information to WikiLeaks?
2. According to Walker, what is Cryptome?
3. At what point do many people believe that WikiLeaks went too far, according to Walker?

You won't find WikiLeaks' biggest impact in any specific story the site has exposed. You'll find it in the bracing fear of what the place might publish next. That anxiety, more than anything else, explains the arrest of Bradley Manning, the soldier who allegedly leaked that infamous video of the airstrikes that killed two Reuters employees in Baghdad. The government doesn't want to deal with a world where a disillusioned functionary can spill secrets so easily, and it's doing everything it can to bring back the days when leaking a story was far harder.

What Is WikiLeaks?

For those who tuned in late: WikiLeaks is an online operation that lets whistleblowers publish damaging documents without anyone—not even the people who run the website—learning who the leaker is. Besides the Baghdad footage, its revelations have ranged from the emails that set off the Climategate scandal to the Standard Operating Procedures manual from the U.S. prison at Guantanamo Bay. The authorities arrested Manning after he told an informant that he had sent the site the video and a trove of other damaging information, including thousands of U.S. diplomatic cables. The cables have not yet materialized, and WikiLeaks co-founder Julian Assange says he doesn't have them.

It's not yet clear that Manning actually *is* the leaker, as opposed to merely being a braggart. But I hope he avoids a jail term either way. The Obama administration has brought an ugly double standard to the misdeeds committed during the Bush years. It has passed up opportunities to prosecute those crimes on the grounds that it wants "to look forward and not backwards," but it has shown no such restraint when it comes to prosecuting the people who exposed those crimes in the first place. Having brought charges against two other leakers, including NSA whistleblower Thomas Drake, the feds now seem set to do the same thing to Manning. Meanwhile, WikiLeaks itself has been the subject of an Army counterintelligence report, which suggested that "identification, exposure, termination of employment, criminal prosecution, [or] legal action against" whistleblowers could "damage or destroy" the belief that WikiLeaks protects its sources' identities, and will thus "deter others considering similar actions from using the Wikileaks.org Web site." (We know about the report because it appeared—where else?— on WikiLeaks.)

Criticism of WikiLeaks

WikiLeaks has attracted a wide range of criticisms, and not just from the knee-jerk defenders of the institutions it exposes. A similar public disclosure site, Cryptome, has published texts allegedly written by "A WIKILEAKS Insider," who accuses the organization of failing to protect its leakers and of misleading the public about its finances. But most critiques of WikiLeaks boil down to one of two complaints. The first is that it distributes information that shouldn't be spread; the second is that it distributes claims that aren't accurate. Put another way, people complain that it's too truthful and that it isn't truthful enough.

The second criticism hasn't come up as often as you might expect. When WikiLeaks publishes an article analyzing the documents on the site, the writer's claims are dissected and denounced as widely as any other arguments on the Internet. But with rare exceptions, the documents themselves tend to be accepted as legitimate. Pundits may debate the *meaning* of the Baghdad video, the Climategate emails, or the Guantanamo prison manual, but their provenance has been well-established. Given the enemies that WikiLeaks has made, you might expect that by this time

WikiLeaks

WikiLeaks is a nonprofit organization based in Sweden that makes sensitive and classified information available to the public via its website, wikileaks.org. The administrators of the site focus on documents that expose actions they view as criminal or unethical, particularly actions committed by governments or corporations. The material available on WikiLeaks is donated by anonymous individuals. WikiLeaks takes great pains to ensure that those who leak the documents remain anonymous for their own protection, and these donors are often unknown even to the administrators of the site. In the five years following its launch in 2006, WikiLeaks became recognized as one of the world's leading sources of leaked information, and changed the way that many people view modern investigative journalism. By late 2011, however, lack of financial support seemed likely to doom the organization.

"WikiLeaks," Global Issues in Context
Online Collection, *Gale, 2012.*

someone would have attempted to discredit the outfit by feeding it phony data. But if this has been tried, there's no sign yet that the site has taken the bait. As a means of distributing raw information, WikiLeaks works.

Assessing the Risk

For some critics, it works too well. Many people argued that WikiLeaks went too far in 2008, when it posted the technical details of some of the jammers the military had used to stop insurgents from detonating IEDs in Iraq. The decision didn't necessarily put lives in danger—by the time the material appeared, the jammers in question had largely been superceded—but it's hard to see what it was supposed to achieve either. Exposing information can carry risks, and in that case the risk wasn't worth it.

But concealing information can be risky as well. Thanks to WikiLeaks, Chinese citizens have access to information about unrest in Tibet; thanks to WikiLeaks, Kenyans can read about the extrajudicial killings committed by their own police. Thanks to WikiLeaks, we have evidence of corruption in the Kaupthing Bank in Iceland, and of deadly toxic dumping off the coast of Africa. WikiLeaks has expanded our knowledge of how prisoners are treated at Guantanamo, how the CIA tries to manage public opinion in Europe, and how some prominent climate scientists talk about their critics. And if Thomas Drake had revealed the NSA's illicit surveillance program to WikiLeaks instead of the *Baltimore Sun*, he might not be facing a prison sentence today. You can complain about some of the editorial decisions that WikiLeaks' managers have made, but as with the free press in general, we're better off with the site than without it.

WikiLeaks Benefits Society

Above all, we're better off now that the large, hierarchical institutions where potential leakers dwell have one more reason to look over their shoulders. At some point, even the most thick-headed, slow-moving bureaucratic dinosaurs just might recognize that they're living in a new environment, one where corrupt corporations and government agencies are no more able to control the flow of embarrassing information than record companies can control the flow of digital music files. Just as the online MP3 swap meet continued to thrive after downloaders started landing in court and Napster was effectively destroyed, the revolution that WikiLeaks represents won't die even if Manning is imprisoned and Julian Assange's site shuts down. Thanks to the Internet, a new wave of grassroots journalists, and a global network of human rights activists, it's less risky than ever before to release incriminating information anonymously. The result will be a world where it's easier not just to expose misbehavior but to deter it.

> "What WikiLeaks revealed when
> it drew back the curtain is more or
> less what most Americans already
> suspected had been going on, and were
> therefore prepared to tolerate."

The WikiLeaks Scandal Reveals the Limitations of the Public's Desire for Transparency

Alasdair Roberts

Alasdair Roberts is an author and professor of law and public policy at Suffolk University Law School. In the following viewpoint, he asserts that WikiLeaks' massive release of US diplomatic and military documents failed to spark the outrage and calls for political change that the hacktivist collective expected. Instead, he contends that the secret cables and documents confirmed to the US public that its government was willing to act forcefully in the pursuit of US interests overseas. It also ignited a backlash against WikiLeaks, which he argues was viewed as a destabilizing force during an anxious time. Roberts also maintains that the disclosures did not have their intended effect, because many of the revelations were open secrets and did not surprise or shock many Americans.

As you read, consider the following questions:

1. According to Roberts, how many secret documents describing US military operations in Afghanistan from 2004 through 2009 did WikiLeaks release in July 2010?
2. What percentage of the State Department cables that were leaked in 2010 does Roberts say was classified as secret?
3. According to a CNN poll cited in the viewpoint, what percentage of Americans disapproved of WikiLeaks' release of US diplomatic and military documents in December 2010?

L ate last November [2010], the antisecrecy group WikiLeaks achieved the greatest triumph in its short history. A consortium of major news media organizations—including *The New York Times, The Guardian, Der Spiegel, Le Monde,* and *El País*—began publishing excerpts from a quarter-million cables between the U.S. State Department and its diplomatic outposts that WikiLeaks had obtained. The group claimed that the cables constituted "the largest set of confidential documents ever to be released into the public domain." *The Guardian* predicted that the disclosures would trigger a "global diplomatic crisis."

This was the fourth major disclosure orchestrated by WikiLeaks last year. In April, it had released a classified video showing an attack in 2007 by U.S. Army helicopters in the streets of Baghdad that killed 12 people, including two employees of the Reuters news agency. In July, it had collaborated with the news media consortium on the release of 90,000 documents describing U.S. military operations in Afghanistan from 2004 through 2009. These records included new reports of civilian casualties and "friendly fire" incidents. In October came a similar but larger set of documents—almost 400,000—detailing U.S. military operations in Iraq.

Waging a War on Secrecy

WikiLeaks' boosters said that the group was waging a war on secrecy, and by the end of 2010 it seemed to be winning. The leaks marked "the end of secrecy in the old-fashioned, Cold War–era sense," claimed *The Guardian* journalists David Leigh and Luke Harding. A Norwegian politician nominated WikiLeaks for the Nobel Peace Prize, saying that it had helped "redraw the map of information freedom." "Like him or not," wrote a *Time* magazine journalist in December, WikiLeaks founder Julian Assange had "the power to impose his judgment of what should or shouldn't be secret."

Did the leaks of 2010 really mark the end of "old-fashioned secrecy?" Not by a long shot. Certainly, new information technologies have made it easier to leak sensitive information and broadcast it to the world. A generation ago, leaking was limited by the need to physically copy and smuggle actual documents. Now it is a matter of dragging, dropping, and clicking Send. But there are still impressive barriers to the kind of "radical transparency" WikiLeaks says it wants to achieve. Indeed, the WikiLeaks experience shows how durable those barriers are.

Assessing the Impact of WikiLeaks

Let's begin by putting the leaks in proper perspective. A common way of showing their significance is to emphasize the sheer volume of material. In July 2010, *The Guardian* described the release of the Afghan war documents as "one of the biggest leaks in U.S. military history." Assange, an Australian computer programmer and activist who had founded WikiLeaks in 2006 (and is currently in Britain facing extradition to Sweden on rape and sexual molestation charges), compared it to perhaps the most famous leak in history. "The Pentagon Papers was about 10,000 pages," he told the United Kingdom's Channel 4 News, alluding to the secret Pentagon history of America's involvement in Vietnam that was leaked in 1971. By contrast, there were "about 200,000 pages in this material."

The Afghan war logs did not hold the record for long. In October, they were supplanted by the Iraq disclosures, "the greatest data leak in the history of the United States military," according to *Der Spiegel*. Within weeks, WikiLeaks was warning that this record too would soon be shattered. It boasted on Twitter that its next release, the State Department cables, would be "7× the size of the Iraq War Logs." Indeed, it was "an astonishing mountain of words," said the two *Guardian* journalists. "If the tiny memory stick containing the cables had been a set of printed texts, it would have made up a library containing more than 2,000 sizable books."

Gauging the significance of leaks based on document volume involves a logical fallacy. The reasoning is this: If we are in possession of a larger *number* of sensitive documents than ever before, we must also be in possession of a larger *proportion* of the total stockpile than ever before. But this assumes that the total itself has not changed over time.

In fact, the amount of sensitive information held within the national security apparatus is immensely larger than it was a generation ago. Technological change has caused an explosion in the rate of information production within government agencies, as everywhere else. For example, the leaked State Department cables might have added up to about two gigabytes of data—one-quarter of an eight-gigabyte memory card. By comparison, it has been estimated that the outgoing Bush White House transferred 77 terabytes of data to the National Archives in 2009. That is almost 10,000 memory cards for the White House alone. The holdings of other agencies are even larger.

The truth is that a count of leaked messages tells us nothing about the significance of a breach. Only six percent of the State Department cables that were leaked last year were classified as secret. And the State Department has said that the network from which the cables were extracted was not even the primary vehicle for disseminating its information. In the period in which most of the quarter-million WikiLeaks cables were distributed within the U.S. government, a State Department official said, "we disseminated 2.4 million cables, 10 times as many, through other systems."

WikiLeaks Has a Flawed Mission

The 2010 disclosures also revealed fundamental problems with the WikiLeaks project. The logic that initially motivated Assange and his colleagues was straightforward: WikiLeaks would post leaked information on the Internet and rely on the public to interpret it, become outraged, and demand reform. The antisecrecy group, which at the start of last year [2010] had a core of about 40 volunteers, had great faith in the capacity of the public to do the right thing. Daniel Domscheit-Berg, who was WikiLeaks' spokesman until he broke with Assange last fall, explained the reasoning in *Inside WikiLeaks*, a book published earlier this year: "If you provide people sufficient background information, they are capable of behaving correctly and making the right decisions."

This proposition was soon tested and found wanting. When WikiLeaks released a series of U.S. military counterinsurgency manuals in 2008, Domscheit-Berg thought there would be "outrage around the world, and I expected journalists to beat down our doors." The manuals described techniques for preventing the overthrow of governments friendly to the United States. In fact, the reaction was negligible. "No one cared," writes Domscheit-Berg, "because the subject matter was too complex."

Examining the Packaging of Information

As the British journalist John Lanchester recently observed, WikiLeaks' "release of information is unprecedented: But it is not journalism. The data need to be interpreted, studied, made into a story." WikiLeaks attempted to do this itself when it released the Baghdad helicopter video. Assange unveiled the video at a news conference at the National Press Club in Washington, D.C., and packaged it so that its significance would be clear. He titled it *Collateral Murder*. The edited video, WikiLeaks said, provided evidence of "indiscriminate" and "unprovoked" killing of civilians.

Even with this priming, the public reaction was muted. Many people turned on WikiLeaks itself, charging that it had manipu-

WikiLeaks and the April 2010 Helicopter Video

WikiLeaks gained international attention in April 2010 when it released video footage of a controversial incident in the Iraq War. On 12 July 2007, two journalists from the news agency Reuters and an unknown number of Iraqi civilians were killed when two U.S. Apache helicopters fired on a group of suspected insurgents in the district of New Baghdad, and subsequently destroyed a nearby building with missile strikes. Initial reports from the U.S. military labeled all the Iraqi victims as armed insurgents, and portrayed the deaths of the reporters as collateral damage that could not be foreseen. Reuters tried to gain access to video footage of the encounter, but the Pentagon refused to comply. In early 2010, WikiLeaks received an encrypted copy of video footage of the incident taken from a camera on one of the Apache helicopters. After spending several months cracking the encryption and analyzing every frame of the video, the site released two versions of the footage: one 17-minute version known by the title "Collateral Murder," and a 39-minute version that included an additional missile strike. Although some possible weapons are seen in the video, no one is engaged in combat. After the first attack, U.S. soldiers mistakenly identify a wounded journalist and unarmed civilians as threatening targets, and gun them down.

"WikiLeaks," Global Issues in Context
Online Collection, *2012.*

lated the video to bolster its allegations of military misconduct. "This strategy for stirring up public interest was a mistake," Domscheit-Berg agrees. "A lot of people [felt] . . . that they were being led around by the nose."

The release of the Afghan war documents in July 2010 gave WikiLeaks further evidence of its own limitations. The trove of documents was "vast, confusing, and impossible to navigate," according to *The Guardian*'s Leigh and Harding, "an impenetrable forest of military jargon." Furthermore, the logs contained the names of many individuals who had cooperated with the American military and whose lives could be threatened by disclosure. WikiLeaks recognized the need for a "harm minimization" plan but lacked the field knowledge necessary to make good decisions about what should be withheld.

Forming Key Partnerships

By last summer, all of these difficulties had driven WikiLeaks to seek its partnership with news media organizations. The consortium that handled the disclosures last fall provided several essential services for the group. It gave technical assistance in organizing data and provided the expertise needed to decode and interpret records. It opened a channel to government officials for conversation about the implications of disclosing information that WikiLeaks itself was unable to establish. Finally, of course, the news media organizations had the capacity to command public attention. They were trusted by readers and possessed a skill in packaging information that WikiLeaks lacked.

By the end of 2010, it was clear that WikiLeaks' modus operandi had fundamentally changed. It had begun with an unambiguous conception of its role as a receiver and distributor of leaked information. At year's end, it was performing a different function: It still hoped to serve as a trusted receiver of leaks, but it was now working with mainstream news media to decide how—or if—leaked information ought to be published. For WikiLeaks, this involved difficult concessions. "We were no longer in control of the process," Domscheit-Berg later wrote. The outflow of leaked information was now constrained by the newspapers' willingness to invest money and time in sifting through more documents.

For the newspapers that participated in the consortium, the rationale for publishing leaked information was simple. As the *New York Times* explained in an editorial note when the State Department cables were released in November, Americans "have a right to know what is being done in their name." The cables "tell the unvarnished story of how the government makes its biggest decisions." This is the conventional journalistic argument in defense of disclosure, and there is no doubt that the WikiLeaks revelations provided vivid and sometimes disturbing illustrations of the ways in which power is wielded by the United States and its allies.

WikiLeaks itself wanted bigger things to flow from its work. It continued to expect outrage and political action. Assange told Britain's Channel 4 News last July that he anticipated that the release of the Afghan war documents would shift public opinion against the war. There was a similar expectation following release of the Iraq war documents. But these hopes were again disappointed. In some polls, perceptions about the conduct of the Afghan war actually became more favorable after the WikiLeaks release. Meanwhile, opinion about American engagement in Iraq remained essentially unchanged, as it had been for several years.

The Limits of Outrage

There are good reasons why disclosures do not necessarily produce significant changes in policy or politics. Much depends on the context of events. When the Pentagon Papers came out in 1971, they contributed to policy change because a host of other forces were pushing in the same direction. The American public was exhausted by the Vietnam War, which at its peak involved the deployment of almost four times as many troops as are now in Iraq and Afghanistan. Many Americans were also increasingly skeptical of all forms of established authority. The federal government's status was further tarnished by other revelations about abuses of power by the White House, CIA, and FBI.

We live in very different times. There is no popular movement against U.S. military engagement overseas, no broad reaction against established authority in American society, no youth rebellion. The public mood in the United States is one of economic uncertainty and physical insecurity. Many Americans want an assurance that their government is willing and able to act forcefully in the pursuit of U.S. interests. In this climate, the incidents revealed by WikiLeaks—spying on United Nations diplomats, covert military action against terrorists, negotiations with regimes that are corrupt or guilty of human rights abuses—might not even be construed as abuses of power at all. On the contrary, they could be regarded as proof that the U.S. government is prepared to get its hands dirty to protect its citizens.

The Destabilizing Impact of WikiLeaks

Indeed, it could be said that WikiLeaks was doing the one thing Americans least wished for: increasing instability and their sense of anxiety. The more WikiLeaks disclosed last year, the more American public opinion hardened against it. By December, according to a CNN poll, almost 80 percent of Americans disapproved of WikiLeaks' release of U.S. diplomatic and military documents. In a CBS News poll, most respondents said they thought the disclosures were likely to hurt U.S. foreign relations. Three-quarters affirmed that there are "some things the public does not have a right to know if it might affect national security."

As WikiLeaks waited fruitlessly for public outrage, it began to see another obstacle to the execution of its program. WikiLeaks relies on the Internet for the rapid dissemination of leaked information. The assumption, which seemed plausible in the early days of cyberspace, is that the Internet is a vast global commons—a free space that imposes no barrier on the flow of data. But even online, commercial and political considerations routinely compromise the movement of information.

Cutting Off WikiLeaks

This reality was quickly illustrated after the release of the State Department cables on November 28. Three days later, Amazon Web Services, a subsidiary of Amazon.com that rents space for the storage of digitized information, stopped acting as a host for WikiLeaks' material, alleging that the group had violated its terms of service. The same day, a smaller firm that provides online graphics capabilities, Tableau Software, discontinued its support. The firm that managed WikiLeaks' domain name, EveryDNS. net, also suspended services, so that the domain name wikileaks. org was no longer operable. On December 20, Apple removed an application from its online store that offered iPhone and iPad users access to the State Department cables.

All of these actions complicated WikiLeaks' ability to distribute leaked information. Decisions by other organizations also undermined its financial viability. Five days after the State Department disclosures, PayPal, which manages online payments, announced that it would no longer process donations to WikiLeaks, alleging that the group had violated its terms of service by encouraging or facilitating illegal activity. MasterCard and Visa Europe soon followed suit.

Critics alleged that these firms were acting in response to political pressure, and many American legislators did in fact call on businesses to break with WikiLeaks. But direct political pressure was hardly necessary; cold commercial judgment led to the same decision. WikiLeaks produced little revenue for any of these businesses but threatened to entangle all of them in public controversy. A public-relations specialist told Seattle's KIRO News that it was "bizarre" for Amazon to assist WikiLeaks during a holiday season: "I don't think you mix politics with retail." Worse still, businesses were exposed to cyberattacks by opponents of WikiLeaks within the hacker community that disrupted their relationships with other, more profitable clients.

These business decisions hurt WikiLeaks significantly. Assange said they amounted to "economic censorship" and claimed that actions by these financial intermediaries were costing Wiki-Leaks $650,000 per week in lost donations.

The U.S. Government's Response

The leaks also provoked a vigorous reaction by the U.S. government. The Army came down hard on Private Bradley Manning, the apparent source of all four of the 2010 disclosures, bringing 34 charges against him. The most serious of these, aiding the enemy, could result in a death sentence, although prosecutors have said they will not seek one. The government is also investigating other individuals in connection with the leaks. Some in Congress have used the episodes to argue for strengthening the law on unauthorized disclosure of national security information, and federal agencies have tightened administrative controls on access to sensitive information. These steps, which may well produce a result precisely the opposite of what WikiLeaks intends by reducing citizens' access to information about the government, have been taken by an administration that promised on its first day in office to "usher in a new era of open government."

The Problem with WikiLeaks

WikiLeaks is predicated on the assumption that the social order—the set of structures that channel and legitimize power—is both deceptive and brittle: deceptive in the sense that most people who observe the social order are unaware of the ways in which power is actually used, and brittle in the sense that it is at risk of collapse once people are shown the true nature of things. The primary goal, therefore, is revelation of the truth. In the past it was difficult to do this, mainly because primitive technologies made it difficult to collect and disseminate damning information. But now these technological barriers are gone. And once information is set free, the theory goes, the world will change.

We have seen some of the difficulties with this viewpoint. Even in the age of the Internet, there is no such thing as the instantaneous and complete revelation of the truth. In its undigested form, information often has no transformative power at all. Raw data must be distilled and interpreted, and the attention of a distracted audience must be captured. The process by which this is done is complex and easily influenced by commercial and governmental interests. This was true before the advent of the Internet and remains true today.

Beyond this, there is a final and larger problem. It may well be that many of the things WikiLeaks imagines are secrets are not really secrets at all. It may be that what WikiLeaks revealed when it drew back the curtain is more or less what most Americans already suspected had been going on, and were therefore prepared to tolerate.

Releasing Open Secrets

To put it another way, much of what WikiLeaks has released might best be described as open secrets. It would have been no great shock to most Americans, for example, to learn about the United States' covert activities against terrorists in Yemen. "The only surprising thing about the WikiLeaks revelations is that they contain no surprises," says the noted Slovenian philosopher Slavoj Žižek, a professor at the European Graduate School. "The real disturbance was at the level of appearances: We can no longer pretend we don't know what everyone knows we know."

In a sense, it was odd to expect that there would be great surprises. The diplomatic and national security establishment of the U.S. government employs millions of people. Most of the critical decisions about the development of foreign policy, and about the apparatus necessary to execute that policy, have been made openly by democratically elected leaders, and sanctioned by voters in national elections over the course of 60 years. In broad terms, Americans know how U.S. power is exercised, and for what purpose. And so there are limits to what WikiLeaks can unveil. Even *New York Times* executive editor Bill Keller conceded that the disclosures did not "expose some deep, unsuspected perfidy in high places." They provide only "texture, nuance, and drama."

None of this is an argument for complacency about government secrecy. Precisely because of the scale and importance of the national security apparatus, it ought to be subjected to close scrutiny. Existing oversight mechanisms such as freedom of information laws and declassification policies are inadequate and should be strengthened. The monitoring capacity of news media outlets and other nongovernmental organizations must be enhanced. And citizens should be encouraged to engage more deeply in debates about the aims and methods of U.S. foreign policy. All of these steps involve hard work. There is no technological quick fix. A major difficulty with the WikiLeaks project is that it may delude us into believing otherwise.

> *"Information technology allows small actors such as Julian Assange to wreak previously unimagined destruction on U.S. national security through cyberspace."*

WikiLeaks Is an Unprecedented Threat to US National Security

Marc A. Thiessen

Marc A. Thiessen is an author and political columnist. In the following viewpoint, he contends that WikiLeaks has declared war on the United States by committing cybersabotage and releasing hundreds of thousands of secret cables and classified diplomatic and military documents. Such disclosures, he maintains, are an unprecedented threat to US national security and should be treated as such. Thiessen argues that US officials should rally a coalition of governments to shut down their servers and cut off the group's finances. Also, he asserts, the US Department of Defense should unleash an army of cyberwarriors to attack the WikiLeaks website and disrupt its activities at every level.

As you read, consider the following questions:

1. How did Hillary Clinton describe the disclosure of hundreds of thousands of classified diplomatic and military documents in 2010, according to Thiessen?
2. What country does Thiessen say is forcing the company OVH SAS to stop hosting WikiLeaks?
3. What hacker does Thiessen identify as the one who successfully crashed the WikiLeaks website repeatedly in 2010?

Secretary of State Hillary Clinton got one thing right last week [December 2010]—she described WikiLeaks' disclosure of hundreds of thousands of classified documents as "an attack." Indeed, it was the third such attack in five months that WikiLeaks has launched against the United States and its international partners. WikiLeaks itself has described its struggle in military terms. Founder Julian Assange recently posted a Tweet from one of his supporters declaring: "The first serious infowar is now engaged. The field of battle is WikiLeaks. You are the troops."

Declaring Cyberwar

Like the war on terror, we have been attacked in this new cyber war in ways we did not anticipate. Over the past decade, the U.S. government has spent billions to stop foreign adversaries from remotely penetrating our computer networks for sabotage. Instead of trying to break through these defenses, Assange pioneered a new form of cyber sabotage. He found someone who allegedly penetrated our classified systems from within, downloaded America's secrets onto a Lady Gaga CD and gave them to Assange, who then disseminated this stolen information across the world.

Assange has made clear he intends to continue posting stolen classified information and has effectively dared the United States and the world to try and stop him. He recently announced

"Diplomacy and Wikileaks." © 2010 Paresh Nath, Cagle Cartoons.

through his lawyer that if he is arrested, he will unleash a "thermonuclear device" of completely unexpurgated government files. Think about that: Assange has threatened America with the cyber equivalent of thermonuclear war.

If WikiLeaks is treating this as a war in cyberspace, America should do the same. The first step is to rally a coalition of the willing to defeat WikiLeaks by shutting down its servers and cutting off its finances. WikiLeaks' most recent disclosures—which exposed not only America's secrets but also those of other nations—seem to have awakened others to the threat the group poses.

Fighting WikiLeaks

In recent days, WikiLeaks has had trouble staying online—in part because governments have been pressuring companies to stop hosting WikiLeaks. In the United States, Amazon.com kicked

WikiLeaks off of its servers after an aide to Joe Lieberman, chairman of the Senate Homeland Security and Governmental Affairs Committee, complained. Another U.S. provider, EveryDNS.net, kicked WikiLeaks off as well, and PayPal.com cut off the account WikiLeaks had been using to collect donations.

In France, Industry Minister Eric Besson said the government would force a French company, OVH SAS, to stop hosting WikiLeaks, declaring, "France cannot host Internet sites that violate the secrets of diplomatic relations and endanger people protected by diplomatic secrecy." Other countries should be encouraged to follow suit.

As WikiLeaks is driven from the cyber territory of responsible countries, it will seek refuge elsewhere on the Internet, setting up operations in nations where it believes it will receive protection. Governments that provide WikiLeaks with virtual safe havens should be told in no uncertain terms: "You are either with us, or you are with WikiLeaks." If they refuse to shut WikiLeaks down on their territory, action should be taken to drive WikiLeaks from those safe havens.

Unleash the Hacktivists

Last week, a Pentagon spokesman confirmed that the United States does in fact have the offensive capabilities in cyberspace to take down WikiLeaks, but that the Obama administration chose not to use them. This failure to act prompted a patriotic hacker who goes by the name th3j35t3r (the Jester) to attack WikiLeaks himself, repeatedly taking down its Web site.

If "one guy with a laptop" can shut down WikiLeaks even temporarily, imagine what the 1,100 cyber-warriors at U.S. Cyber Command could do. While the United States sits on the sidelines, the *New York Times* reported Saturday that WikiLeaks had come under assault "from armies of zombie computers in Europe, Russia and Asia." This flood of attacks creates the perfect cover for the United States to deliver the coup de grâce to WikiLeaks secretly, with no fingerprints, if it chose to do so.

Some say attacking WikiLeaks would be fruitless. Really? In the past year, the Iranian nuclear system has been crippled by a computer worm called "Stuxnet," which has attacked Iran's industrial systems and the personal computers of Iranian nuclear scientists. To this day, no one has traced the origin of the worm. Imagine the impact on WikiLeaks's ability to distribute additional classified information if its systems were suddenly and mysteriously infected by a worm that would fry the computer of anyone who downloaded the documents. WikiLeaks would probably have very few future visitors to its Web site.

WikiLeaks represents a new and unprecedented cyber threat that cannot be ignored or wished away. Just as terrorism allows small groups of individuals to wreak destruction on a scale that was once the province of nation-states, information technology allows small actors such as Julian Assange to wreak previously unimagined destruction on U.S. national security through cyberspace. This is a threat that requires a U.S. response. Hillary Clinton is right—WikiLeaks has attacked America. The only question is: Will America return fire?

> *"If Wikileaks is doing a disservice by indiscriminately airing classified dirty laundry, the U.S. government is doing its public a disservice by keeping this kind of information . . . secret."*

A Defense of Wikileaks

John B. Judis

John B. Judis is the senior editor of the New Republic. *In the following viewpoint, he offers a defense of WikiLeaks by suggesting that it is performing an invaluable service by making key information on US foreign policy public. Judis argues that the WikiLeaks disclosure of classified US diplomatic and military information has the potential to improve US foreign policy by exposing US imperialism in the Middle East. These revelations provide the opportunity to examine US actions in that region, Judis concludes.*

As you read, consider the following questions:

1. In what year were the Pentagon Papers released, according to Judis?
2. According to Judis, when did Britain announce its withdrawal from the Middle East?

3. What does Judis contend that the United States demonstrated in 2003 as related to the Middle East?

The Obama administration has condemned Wikileaks for its second release within a year of classified foreign policy documents. And some liberal commentators have backed up the administration's complaints. And I am not going to argue that the administration doesn't have a case. Governments rely on candid assessments from their diplomats; and if Americans in overseas embassies have to assume that they are writing for the general public and not for their superiors back home, they are not likely to be very candid. But there is also something to be said in defense of Wikileaks. Or to put it in the most minimal terms, there is a reason why, outside of Washington, most people, and much of the respectable press, have focused on the contents of these leaks rather than on the manner in which they were leaked.

Many of the cables consist of high-level gossip, or educated but not necessarily insightful opinion, with little bearing on policy. Yet those that do deal with policy reveal contradictions between what the Bush or Obama administrations have been telling the public and what was known inside the State Department and White House. For instance, while the White House was warning Congress that Iran was arming the Taliban in Afghanistan, Secretary of Defense Robert Gates was assuring the Italian foreign minister that "there was little lethal material crossing the Afghanistan-Iranian border."

Other revelations bear upon what the administration knew or thought it knew about other countries, but was not telling the public. Some of the most significant concern China. The State Department believed that the Chinese government was behind the global computer hacking that affected not only Google in China, but American Defense Department computers. The Chinese have also rebuffed American pleas to stop exporting militarily sensitive equipment to Iran and North Korea.

Should this kind of information be known to the public? The administration says it should not. Referring to the leak about China and proliferation, a "senior administration official" told the *Washington Post*, "Clearly, you don't want any information like this leaked illegally and disseminated to the public." But I beg to differ. I think the public has a right to know about China's willingness to arm Iran and North Korea. And I applaud Wikileaks for making *this* kind of material public. I would feel the same way if an enterprising reporter unearthed the relevant documents and published them in the *New York Times*. If Wikileaks is doing a disservice by indiscriminately airing classified dirty laundry, the U.S. government is doing its public a disservice by keeping this kind of information about China or Iran or about Afghanistan's government secret.

There is another consideration—one that bears on the history of these kind of leaks. These Wikileaks revelations are the third major episode of this type which occurred during the past century. The first was the new Bolshevik government's release in 1917 of secret treaties signed by Great Britain, France, and Czarist Russia during World War I. The second was the Pentagon Papers in 1971. They have something in common. Each was— and I use the word advisedly, and will explain how—a protest against great power imperialism.

On November 26, 1917, the new Bolshevik government of Russia released copies of the secret wartime agreements between Russia, France, and Great Britain. The most sensational of these was the Sykes-Picot agreement of 1916 to divide up the Ottoman Middle East after World War I. The revelations were shocking in the Middle East, but also in the United States, where many blamed European imperial ambitions for the onset of the Great War.

The Pentagon Papers, which Daniel Ellsberg released to the *New York Times*, laid bare the secret history of the Vietnam war. It revealed that the Kennedy and Johnson administrations had consistently lied to the public about the aims and scope of

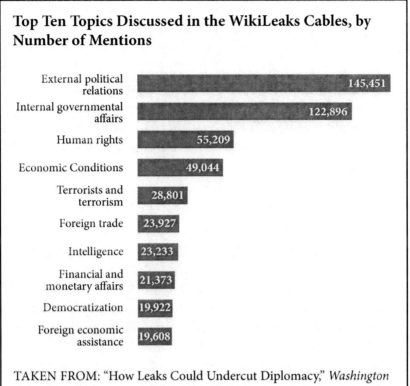

Top Ten Topics Discussed in the WikiLeaks Cables, by Number of Mentions

Topic	Number of Mentions
External political relations	145,451
Internal governmental affairs	122,896
Human rights	55,209
Economic Conditions	49,044
Terrorists and terrorism	28,801
Foreign trade	23,927
Intelligence	23,233
Financial and monetary affairs	21,373
Democratization	19,922
Foreign economic assistance	19,608

TAKEN FROM: "How Leaks Could Undercut Diplomacy," *Washington Post*, November 30, 2011. www.washingtonpost.com.

American intervention, which, it turned out, had little to do with professed aim of spreading or protecting democracy in Southeast Asia. The Wikileaks have primarily been concerned with exposing American intervention in the Middle East and neighboring Afghanistan.

Imperialism? Many Americans hoped that World War I would end the age of imperialism that had led to much of Asia and Africa being divvied up into colonies, protectorates and spheres of influence. But as Lenin would correctly note in his wartime polemic, *Imperialism*, the conflict was in fact a war of imperial redivision. And the Sykes-Picot agreement and what happened after the war proved that to be the case.

After the war, the great powers resorted to various subterfuges (for instance, League of Nations mandates) to maintain their hold over new or former colonies; or they adopted a neo-imperial strategy pioneered by the British in Egypt of fostering client states staffed by locals, but under the quiet control of their embassies. If the locals didn't do as they were told, the troops were brought in. It wasn't imperialism in the sense that the word began to be used in the 1880s, but it was a continuation of the age of empire.

These forms of great power intervention lingered in Latin America, Asia, and Africa, as well as Eastern Europe, in the decades after World War II, but they disappeared by the end of cold war, except in the Middle East, where they endured due to the importance of oil to the world economy and to national militaries. When the United States became the principal outside power in the region after the British announced their withdrawal in February 1947, it also assumed a version of the British neo-imperial strategy.

The United States does not have colonies in the region, but it does have client states, or protectorates, whose governments it defends and sometimes sustains in exchange for access to their oil, or in exchange to their acquiescence to American objectives in the region. As the United States demonstrated in January 1991, it will go to war to protect these states. Or as it demonstrated in 2003, it will go to war to punish nations that defy it. American relations with these states, most of which have autocratic regimes, has largely had to be conducted in secret for fear of inflaming the regime's subjects, many of whom resent their control. So in this respect, secret diplomacy has remained endemic. And the Wikileaks revelations are in the spirit of past attempts to expose the older imperialism and its newer variations.

Is this kind of intervention a worthy target for these kind of leaks—the way that the Sykes-Picot agreement or the war in Vietnam was? After World War II, the United States justified its interventionism on the grounds of cold war necessity;

and recently it has invoked the threat of radical Islamic terror. Radical Islam and its war against the United States can in turn be traced to American support for oil autocracies—Al Qaeda was borne out of opposition to American bases on Saudi soil—and America's extensive support for Israel. Does America need to create client states in Iraq and Afghanistan in order to protect its citizens from Al Qaeda? Or from other threats? I am not going to get into these questions, but the fact that they *are* questions indicates why so many people around the world have been more focused on the Wikileaks rather than the Wikileaker.

> *"America's cyber warriors have not yet mastered their trade."*

The WikiLeaks Scandal Reveals the US Government Lacks the Will to Deal with Cyberthreats

Cliff May

Cliff May is a journalist, political commentator, and the president of the Foundation for the Defense of Democracies. In the following viewpoint, he questions the US response to the disclosure of hundreds of thousands of secret diplomatic cables and classified documents by WikiLeaks. May contends that US officials should have taken better measures to prevent the fiasco in the first place. Once WikiLeaks published the information, May argues that the US government should have unleashed a devastating computer virus to bring down the WikiLeaks servers. He concludes that the ineffectual US response shows the government's unwillingness to deal with cyberthreats like WikiLeaks and underscores the need for a strong, cohesive strategy to meet the challenge of the cyber arms race.

As you read, consider the following questions:

1. Who does May identify as the military private who leaked classified information to WikiLeaks?

Cliff May, "Cyber Threats: US Response to WikiLeaks Surprisingly Weak," *Gleaner*, December 9, 2010. Copyright © 2010 by Cliff May. All rights reserved. Reproduced by permission.

2. What did Mike McConnell tell a US Senate committee about the threat of cyberattacks, according to May?

3. According to May, what is Stuxnet?

The theft of hundreds of thousands of secret diplomatic cables and military reports was an act of espionage and treachery. Their release was an act of sabotage. The U.S. government's response to both has been frighteningly feckless.

First and most obviously, how is it possible that those responsible for security at the Departments of Defense and State did not foresee—and take measures that would have prevented—a 22-year-old Army private [Bradley Manning] not just from accessing but also downloading such classified information?

Officials up to and including the Secretary of State have said that the government was just attempting to break down the walls between various agencies. Credible? Not even close.

The U.S. Government Offers a Weak Response

Second, after the first WikiLeaks document dump back in July [2010], why did a computer worm or virus not find its way into WikiLeak servers and destroy them? Yes, that would have caused an uproar in some quarters. So what? Government spokesmen would do the one thing they know how to do: deny complicity or simply refuse comment.

Instead, Pentagon spokesmen are saying it's not that the U.S. lacks the means to put WikiLeaks out of business but that such a response would have been excessive in this particular instance. Really?

As satisfying as it is for national security hawks like me to have hard evidence that Arab leaders are terrified by the prospect of nuclear-armed Jihadis in Tehran—and are demanding that America "cut off the head of the snake"—the fact is these disclosures will be hugely damaging to U.S. diplomatic efforts.

But the alternative explanation is that America's cyber warriors have not yet mastered their trade. If you don't grasp how consequential that is, listen to Mike McConnell who served as director of the National Security Agency under President Bill Clinton and as director of National Intelligence under President George W. Bush. Earlier this year, he told a Senate committee that the threat of cyber attacks "rivals nuclear weapons in terms of seriousness."

Cyberattacks Are a Dire Threat

That's because enemy cyber combatants are developing cyber weapons that could shut down our electrical grid (causing blackouts of indefinite duration) or destroy the electronic records and processes on which our financial systems depend.

China or Russia would probably utilize such a capability only in the event of a serious conflict breaking out with the U.S., which is bad enough.

But Iran for more than three decades has considered itself at war with "the Great Satan." President Mahmoud Ahmadinejad might view such a cyber attack as contributing toward his long-term goal: "A world without America."

Wouldn't we retaliate with a rain of fire? We might not know for certain Iran was responsible. It also is possible that Iran's current rulers wouldn't care if we did. "We do not worship Iran, we worship Allah," the Ayatollah Khomeini, leader of Iran's Islamic Revolution, said in 1980. "For patriotism is another name for paganism. I say let (Iran) burn. I say let this land go up in smoke, provided Islam emerges triumphant in the rest of the world."

Fighting the Cyberwar

Cyberspace is not the battlefield of the future—it's the battlefield of the present. If we didn't know that before we should know that now, thanks to Stuxnet, a computer worm that has worked its way into Iran's nuclear facilities and, encouragingly, done significant damage to them.

The Stuxnet Virus

Just over a year ago, a computer in Iran started repeatedly rebooting itself, seemingly without reason. Suspecting some kind of malicious software (malware), analysts at Virus-BlokAda, an antivirus-software company in Minsk, examined the misbehaving machine over the Internet, and soon found that they were right. Disturbingly so: the code they extracted from the Iranian machine proved to be a previously unknown computer virus of unprecedented size and complexity.

On 17 June 2010, VirusBlokAda issued a worldwide alert that set off an international race to track down what came to be known as Stuxnet: the most sophisticated computer malware yet found and the harbinger of a new generation of cyberthreats. Unlike conventional malware, which does its damage only in the virtual world of computers and networks, Stuxnet would turn out to target the software that controls pumps, valves, generators and other industrial machines.

Sharon Weinberger, "Is This the Start of Cyber Warfare?," Nature, June 9, 2011.

Deductive speculation has led many to the belief that the Israelis developed this sophisticated search-and-destroy device. Did Americans partner with them? I hope so.

In his testimony, McConnell warned that we "lack a cohesive strategy" to meet the challenge of the cyber arms race now under way. Jim Lewis, director of the Center for Strategic and International Studies, has added that three years ago "we probably had our electronic Pearl Harbor. It was an espionage Pearl Harbor. Some unknown foreign power, and honestly, we don't know who it is, broke into the (computer systems of the) Department of Defense, to the Department of State, the

Department of Commerce, probably the Department of Energy, probably NASA."

Since that time, building defenses that enemy cyber combatants cannot breach should have been a top priority for the White House and Congress. Will it become one as a result of the WikiLeaks fiasco? If not, what will it take?

Periodical and Internet Sources Bibliography

The following articles have been selected to supplement the diverse views presented in this chapter.

David Carr

"Is This the WikiEnd?," *New York Times*, November 5, 2011. www .nytimes.com.

Jamais Cascio

"The Internet May Have Upended Traditional Institutions, but It's a Brutal Weapon," *Newsweek*, June 25, 2012. www.thedailybeast .com/content/newsweek.html.

Richard Cohen

"WikiLeaks and the Trouble with Transparency," *Washington Post*, December 6, 2010. www.washing tonpost.com.

Anita Isaacs

"It's Not About Assange," *New York Times*, August 19, 2012. www .nytimes.com.

Anatol Lieven

"Analysis: Impact of WikiLeaks' US Cable Publications," *BBC News*, December 4, 2010. www.bbc.co.uk.

Michael Moore and Oliver Stone

"WikiLeaks and Free Speech," *New York Times*, August 20, 2012. www .nytimes.com.

Evgeny Morozov

"Wiki Rehab," *New Republic*, January 7, 2011. www.tnr.com.

Edward Wasserman

"Assange and WikiLeaks: Time to Ask Some Impertinent Questions," *Huffington Post*, August 26, 2012. www.huffingtonpost.com.

Naomi Wolf

"WikiLeaks, Revolution, and the Lost Cojones of American Journalism," *Huffington Post*, February 4, 2011. www.huffington post.com.

**OPPOSING
VIEWPOINTS®
SERIES**

CHAPTER 4

What Is the Role of Government in Hacking?

Chapter Preface

In June 2010, the Internet erupted with conspiracy theories over the discovery of a destructive and groundbreaking computer virus called Stuxnet. VirusBlokAda, a security firm in Belarus, was the first to identify the virus. A month later, Siemens, the German industrial corporation, warned its customers that a specific piece of its software was the target of the malware. By August 2010, Microsoft reported that 45,000 computers around the world had been infected with the Stuxnet computer virus.

A highly sophisticated computer worm, Stuxnet finds its way into a computer's industrial-control system through infected USB memory sticks, spreads through Microsoft Windows, installs a backdoor control system, and then contacts a server in Malaysia for further instructions. It is capable of shutting down large-scale and complex industrial systems completely. Computer security experts recognized pretty quickly that this was the work of a cyberpower, not just the product of a few independent hackers. Only a few nations would have the capability to develop Stuxnet, with its complex codes and in-depth knowledge of complicated industrial systems.

By September 2010, computer security specialists were theorizing that Stuxnet was a cyberweapon created to take out one specific target: Iran's uranium-enrichment plant in Natanz. For years, the international community has raised concerns over Iran's determination to develop its nuclear-energy capabilities and build a nuclear bomb. Fears are that Iran's radical Islamic leadership will turn such weapons on Israel and other targets. To hinder these efforts, the international community has imposed harsh economic sanctions on Iran in hopes that it will slow down or even eliminate its uranium enrichment, a key step in creating nuclear energy and weapons.

The evidence certainly seemed to support the theory that the Natanz facility was the target. An analysis of Stuxnet by

Symantec, a computer security company, found that 80 percent of the infected computers were in Iran. Security experts connected the cyberattack with Natanz because of reports that the facility had been experiencing major technical problems since 2009. This was confirmed when it was announced in November 2010 that the situation had been so catastrophic that the Natanz facility was forced to shut down thousands of its centrifuges for long periods in early 2009, stopping the enrichment of uranium and slowing Iran's nuclear program significantly.

On November 29, 2010, Iranian President Mahmoud Ahmadinejad admitted for the first time that Iran's nuclear capability had been crippled by Stuxnet. "They succeeded in creating problems for a limited number of our centrifuges with the software they had installed in electronic parts," Ahmadinejad told reporters at a news conference. "They did a bad thing. Fortunately our experts discovered that and today they are not able [to do that] anymore."

The United States and Israel were identified as likely suspects, because both countries had the necessary cyberweapons expertise to develop the highly sophisticated Stuxnet computer worm. Speculation quickly focused on the United States as the most likely mastermind. In 2011, Iran accused the United States of launching the cyberattack. By 2012, highly credible reports surfaced that Stuxnet was the result of a US government effort, code-name Olympic Games, developed during the administration of George W. Bush and continued under President Barack Obama to cripple the computer systems that ran Iran's nuclear-enrichment facilities. Officially, the United States has denied being the perpetrator of the attack, but it is widely accepted in international circles that it did. It seems to be the first time that United States has used cyberweapons to cripple another country's infrastructure.

The Stuxnet cyberattack raises a number of questions about the role of government in hacking, many of which are examined in the following chapter. The viewpoints touch on issues such as how governments should respond to coordinated and destructive cyberattacks, the importance of cybersecurity legislation, and how government regulations would affect the private sector's ability to protect itself from cyberattacks.

> "The Department [of Defense]
> recognizes that a nation possessing
> sophisticated and powerful cyber
> capabilities could attempt to affect the
> strategic calculus of the United States."

Cyberattacks Require a Military Response

US Department of Defense

The Department of Defense (DoD) is the US government agency responsible for national security and the US military. In the following viewpoint, DoD outlines its strategy for responding to cyberthreats against the United States. The agency offers its support of the US government's stated policy to work with other nations to encourage responsible behavior and thwart those who seek to disrupt US computer networks and disable infrastructure. Deterrence is the first option, the DoD asserts, adding that it will work with all government agencies to discourage potential hackers from launching malicious cyberattacks. However, once an attack is initiated, the DoD contends that it has the right to respond to hostile acts in cyberspace as they would to any other threat and that includes cyberwarfare and military action. In fact, the agency explains, any government that considers launching a crip-

"Department of Defense Cyberspace Policy Report," United States Department of Defense, November 2011.

pling cyberattack on the United States would be warned that the president will respond militarily in order to protect US national security.

As you read, consider the following questions:
1. When was the *International Strategy for Cyberspace* published, according to the viewpoint?
2. What two interagency partners does the DoD say it will continue to work with in order to address threats to the United States?
3. Which two communities does the DoD indicate it works with to secure the best possible intelligence about potential adversaries' cybercapabilities?

The President's [Barack Obama] May 2011 *International Strategy for Cyberspace* states that the United States will, along with other nations, encourage responsible behavior and oppose those who would seek to disrupt networks and systems, dissuading and deterring malicious actors, and reserving the right to defend these national security and vital national assets as necessary and appropriate. When warranted, we will respond to hostile acts in cyberspace as we would to any other threat to our country. All states possess an inherent right to self-defense, and we reserve the right to use all necessary means—diplomatic, informational, military, and economic—to defend our Nation, our Allies, our partners, and our interests. In doing so, we will exhaust all options prior to using force whenever we can; we will carefully weigh the costs and risks of action against the costs of inaction; and we will act in a way that reflects our values and strengthens our legitimacy, seeking broad international support wherever possible. For its part, DoD [Department of Defense] will ensure that the U.S. military continues to have all necessary capabilities in cyberspace to defend the United States and its interests, as it does across all domains.

Deterring Cyberattacks

Deterrence in cyberspace, as with other domains, relies on two principal mechanisms: denying an adversary's objectives and, if necessary, imposing costs on an adversary for aggression. Accordingly, DoD will continue to strengthen its defenses and support efforts to improve the cybersecurity of our government, critical infrastructure, and Nation. By denying or minimizing the benefit of malicious activity in cyberspace, the United States will discourage adversaries from attacking or exploiting our networks. DoD supports these efforts by enhancing our defenses, increasing our resiliency, and conducting military-to-military bilateral and multilateral discussions.

In addition, the U.S. is working with like-minded nations to establish an environment of expectations, or norms of behavior, that increase understanding of cyber doctrine, and guide Allied policies and international partnerships. At the same time, should the "deny objectives" element of deterrence not prove adequate, DoD maintains, and is further developing, the ability to respond militarily in cyberspace and in other domains. Continuing to improve our ability to attribute attacks is a key to military response options.

Government Collaboration Is Vital

Defending the Homeland is an important element of deterrence. DoD will use its significant capability and expertise in support of a whole-of-government approach to protect the Nation. The policy and legal authorities governing DoD's domestic activities— such as Defense Support to Civil Authorities—extend to cyber operations, as they would in any other domain. DoD will continue to work closely with its interagency partners, including the Departments of Justice and Homeland Security, to address threats to the United States from wherever they originate, through a whole-of-government approach. The Department is dedicated to the protection of the Nation, and to the privacy and the civil liberties of its citizens.

Deterrence is a whole-of-government proposition. DoD supports the White House Cybersecurity legislative proposal to protect the American people, U.S. critical infrastructure, and our government's networks and systems more effectively. DoD is working closely with its interagency partners, including the Department of Homeland Security, to increase the cybersecurity of our critical infrastructure. Moreover, DoD continues to work with private sector partners through efforts like the Enduring Security Framework and the Defense Industrial Base Cybersecurity/Information Assurance programs to enhance cybersecurity, reduce vulnerabilities, and encourage the innovation necessary to protect and strengthen the U.S. economy. DoD is working with the Department of State to strengthen ties with our Allies and international partners to enhance mutual security.

Confronting Serious Cyberthreats

[It is necessary to preserve] the President's freedom of action in crises and confrontations involving nations which may pose a manageable conventional threat to the United States but which in theory could pose a serious threat to the U.S. economy, government, or military through cyber attacks.

The Department recognizes that a nation possessing sophisticated and powerful cyber capabilities could attempt to affect the strategic calculus of the United States. In this scenario, an adversary might act in ways antithetical to vital U.S. national interests and attempt to prevent the President from exercising traditional national security options by threatening or implying the launch of a crippling cyber attack against the United States.

Any state attempting such a strategy would be taking a grave risk. DoD recognizes the vital importance of maintaining the President's freedom of action. The Department is working, with our interagency partners, to ensure no future adversaries are tempted to pursue such a strategy. Our efforts focus on the following three areas:

- First, the Department, in conjunction with the Intelligence Community and Law Enforcement agencies, strives to secure the best possible intelligence about potential adversaries' cyber capabilities. These efforts are crucial because the United States needs to understand other nations' cyber capabilities in order to defend against them and to improve our ability to attribute any cyber attacks that may occur. Forensic analysis is a part of attributing attacks, but foreign intelligence collection and international law enforcement cooperation play a key role. In this regard, the co-location of the National Security Agency and United States Cyber Command (USCYBERCOM) provides benefits and efficiencies to the Department for its cyber operations. The National Security Agency's unique strengths and capabilities provide USCYBERCOM with critical cryptologic support for target and access development, enabling DoD cyberspace operations planning and execution.

- Second, the Department recognizes that strong cyber defenses and resilient information architectures, particularly those connected to critical infrastructure, mitigate the ability of a future adversary to constrain the President's freedom of action. If future adversaries are unable to cripple our centers of gravity, they will be more likely to understand that the President has the full menu of national security options available.

- Finally, the President reserves the right to respond using all necessary means to defend our Nation, our Allies, our partners, and our interests from hostile acts in cyberspace. Hostile acts may include significant cyber attacks directed against the U.S. economy, government or military. As directed by the President, response options may include using cyber and/or kinetic capabilities provided by DoD.

> "The real obstacle to making sensible
> cybersecurity policy is hysteria, which
> drowns out common sense."

A Military Response to Cyberattacks Is Unwarranted and Inappropriate

Benjamin H. Friedman and Christopher Preble

Benjamin H. Friedman is a research fellow in defense and homeland security studies, and Christopher Preble is director of foreign policy studies at the Cato Institute. In the following viewpoint, they express their opposition to the US government's stated policy of responding to major cyberattacks with military action. Friedman and Preble view such a policy as an overreaction and unwarranted considering the other options on the table. They argue that the media hypes the threat of cyberattacks to garner readers, and US officials exaggerate it to justify bloated budgets and feed the growing cybersecurity sector. Instead, they conclude, officials should work to calm public fears and avoid threats that can escalate conflicts and limit future flexibility.

As you read, consider the following questions:

1. How did Carl Levin describe a possible cyberattack on the United States, according to the authors?

2. The cyberwar involves which two of the media's favorite subjects, as stated by the authors?

3. According to Friedman and Preble, how much will the federal government spend in 2011 on IT (information technology)?

According to the *Wall Street Journal*, the Pentagon's first cyber security strategy will say that cyberattacks can be acts of war meriting retaliatory military attack. The policy threatens to repeat the overreaction and needless conflict that plagued American foreign policy in the past decade. It builds on national hysteria about threats to cybersecurity, the latest bogeyman to justify our bloated national security state. A wiser approach would put the threat in context to calm public fears and avoid threats that diminish future flexibility.

Defining Cyberattack

A key challenge in responding to "cyberattacks" is defining that term. Reporters sometimes use it to describe hackers stealing credit card numbers or intellectual property. Website vandalism and denial-of-service attacks, where attackers flood websites with requests to overburden and disable them, are often included. Electronic espionage, including the theft of intellectual property or state secrets, also qualifies. More obvious kinds of cyberattack include attacks on military communication systems and hacking that sabotages infrastructure like electricity grids, water systems, or online banking.

The idea of responding militarily to most of these threats is preposterous. We thwart hackers with better passwords, IT professionals and policing, not aircraft carriers. We do not threaten to bomb countries caught spying on us in traditional ways and should not do so just because the prefix "cyber" applies.

The Pentagon will reportedly avoid this definitional difficulty with a policy of "equivalence," where only cyberattacks creating destruction on par with traditional military attacks qualify as acts of war. The trouble is that some acts of war, like naval blockades, damage only commerce. The same goes for all reported cyberattacks. Launching a war to retaliate for a non-lethal attack seems disproportionate, especially where it is unclear whether the attacker served the government. Taken literally, the new policy might have us risking nuclear exchange with Russia because it failed to stop teenagers in Moscow Internet cafés from attacking Citibank.com.

Threats of Cyberattacks Are Exaggerated

The real obstacle to making sensible cybersecurity policy is hysteria, which drowns out common sense. Cyberattacks have never killed an American, yet Senator Carl Levin compared them to weapons of mass destruction. His colleague Jay Rockefeller said they "can shut this country down." Mike McConnell, the former director of national intelligence, called cyberattacks on financial systems "the equivalent of today's nuclear weapon."

These claims rely on the assertions of authorities like White House official-turned-security-consultant Richard Clarke. In a book that *Wired* reviewed under the title "File Under Fiction," Clarke and a co-author suggest that hackers could plunge our nation into chaos in minutes by shutting off power, crashing planes, flooding dams and shutting down stock trading. They obscure the fact that managers of that infrastructure prevent such catastrophes by decoupling it from the public Internet and having backup systems. Clarke ignores evidence showing that hackers have never caused a power outage, and that people rarely panic and loot when the lights go out.

We exaggerate online threats for the same reason we exaggerate other security threats: our information about the danger comes largely from those that benefit from the provision of defenses against it.

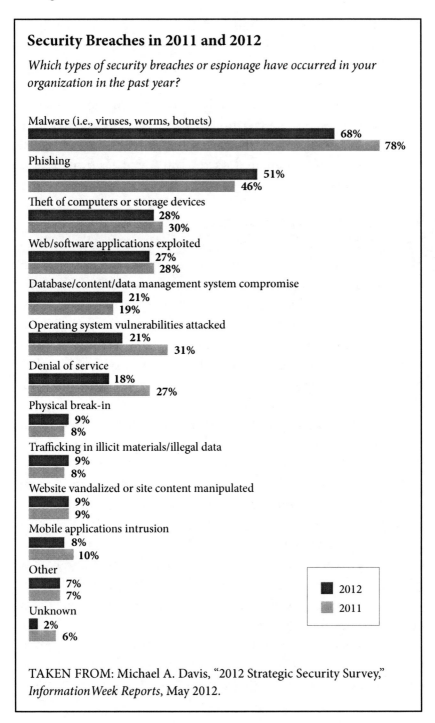

Security Breaches in 2011 and 2012

Which types of security breaches or espionage have occurred in your organization in the past year?

Malware (i.e., viruses, worms, botnets)
68%
78%

Phishing
51%
46%

Theft of computers or storage devices
28%
30%

Web/software applications exploited
27%
28%

Database/content/data management system compromise
21%
19%

Operating system vulnerabilities attacked
21%
31%

Denial of service
18%
27%

Physical break-in
9%
8%

Trafficking in illicit materials/illegal data
9%
8%

Website vandalized or site content manipulated
9%
9%

Mobile applications intrusion
8%
10%

Other
7%
7%

Unknown
2%
6%

2012
2011

TAKEN FROM: Michael A. Davis, "2012 Strategic Security Survey," *Information Week Reports*, May 2012.

The media will print almost any claim about cyberwar, which combines two of its favorite subjects: disaster and the Internet. Pundits and ambitious officials know that doomsday predictions about the next big thing bring attention, promotions and contracting gigs. There is less reward in noting that the Internet heightens economic resilience by making it easier to replace suppliers and distributing information critical to most enterprises.

The Cybersecurity Complex

The $10 billion-plus that the federal government will spend this year on IT security creates a chorus of alarm among contractors and the communities where they park jobs. And agencies involved in cybersecurity—the National Security Agency, the Department of Homeland Security and the Pentagon's Strategic Command, for starters—justify their budgets with cyberalarm.

Competition for power also contributes to the problem. Agencies compete to own cybersecurity policy, as do the Congressional committees that oversee them. Several dozen cybersecurity bills now sit before Congress. Each request for authority, funds or legislative action comes with a claim that inaction leaves us vulnerable.

Cyberfears are not altogether phony. The Internet makes it harder to keep information private, facilitating crimes. Managing the problem requires a mix of liability, regulatory and law enforcement reforms, mostly in state capitals. The federal government has a role to play in securing its networks and secrets, pursuing hackers abroad, reporting on them and developing offensive hacking capabilities. The Stuxnet virus that afflicted Iran's nuclear program demonstrates that U.S. intelligence agencies and those of our allies' are the leading practitioners of cybersabotage. We should keep it that way.

Foreign powers know that killing Americans, whatever the means, will bring retaliation. Reminding them is sensible, but threatening war given vague hypotheticals may simply encourage belligerent decisions in the future. Rather than exaggerate our vulnerabilities, public officials should herald our resilience, noting that most cyberattacks create hassle, not catastrophe, and that our ability to swiftly recover from even the worst attacks is our best defense.

> *"The U.S. should develop a cyber-insurgency doctrine first—then a strategy to implement it."*

The United States Needs to Develop a Smart and Effective Counterinsurgency Strategy for Cyberspace

Paul Rosenzweig

Paul Rosenzweig is a visiting fellow at the Center for Legal and Judicial Studies and the Douglas and Sarah Allison Center for Foreign Policy Studies at the Heritage Foundation. In the following viewpoint, he suggests that the WikiLeaks case has underscored the need for an effective US counterinsurgency strategy in cyberspace. Rosenzweig points out that although there have been a number of cybersecurity strategies, they all focus too much on technology and not enough on a comprehensive approach to addressing the complex and dangerous problem of cyberwarfare. Such a strategy should include a number of elements, he asserts, including collecting human intelligence on non-state actors, government and civilian collaboration, and strengthening the capacity of allies for network security.

As you read, consider the following questions:

1. According to the viewpoint, what did Anonymous call its coordinated attack against major corporations such as Amazon?
2. How can determining the origin of a cyberattack be difficult, as argued by Rosenzweig?
3. According to the author, what is Coreflood?

The tale of WikiLeaks and its founder Julian Assange demonstrates how the U.S. should fight bad actors in cyberspace. WikiLeaks has become a brand name for the disclosure of government secrets. But the more interesting (and less widely remarked upon) part of the story concerns the reaction to Assange's arrest in Great Britain and the decision of many companies (including PayPal, MasterCard, and Amazon.com) to sever financial relationships with his Web site. Their response turned the WikiLeaks fiasco into a kind of cyber war involving a non-state group of commercial actors. The important decisions, however, had nothing do with technology. They were tough calls made by corporate boards reacting responsibly to an irresponsible act. Undermining WikiLeaks's finances likely played a larger role in hindering access to the Web site than any other effort.

The best way to address cyber conflict is to resist the temptation to view it as a one-dimensional contest of "our electrons" versus "their electrons." Like with any conflict, the best strategy is to examine all factors, seeking to exploit one's own strengths and the enemy's weaknesses. This is the same bitter lesson the U.S. learned in Iraq in 2005. During that conflict, the U.S. military faced a small but dedicated group of stateless actors (in that case al-Qaeda operatives and their sympathizers) who used asymmetric means of warfare to harass American troops and to create chaos for the Iraqi government. The U.S. military, in turn, had no doctrine for dealing with countering the influence of these insurgents. Recognizing that gap in doctrinal training, the Army conducted an extended examination of the problem, led by then-Lieutenant Generals David Petraeus and James Amos. The result was a new field manual on counterinsurgency (COIN). The manual advanced the thesis of coordinated military-civilian measures against insurgents—a thesis that now forms the intellectual framework of all U.S. activities in Iraq and Afghanistan. In Iraq, weaning local leaders off support for al-Qaeda arguably had a greater impact in weakening the insurgency than tracking down and killing insurgents.

The approach to warfare that turned back al-Qaeda in Iraq, and the Taliban in Afghanistan, is the right doctrinal solution for winning in cyberspace. The real lesson of the WikiLeaks war is that malfeasant cyber actors behave, in many respects, like insurgents in a kinetic conflict. The methods for confronting these cyber insurgents will be different from those used to confront armed insurgents in the real world, but the principle should be the same. Since 2000, the U.S. government has authored a number of cybersecurity strategies. They all fall short. They have no real doctrinal foundation. They focus too much on technology and not enough on a comprehensive approach to battling cyber insurgency. The U.S. should develop a cyber-insurgency doctrine first—then a strategy to implement it.

The WikiLeaks War

With the disclosure of classified information, WikiLeaks appeared to be launching an assault on state authority (and more particularly, that of the United States, though other governments were also identified). Confronted with WikiLeaks's anti-sovereignty slant, the institutions of traditional commerce soon responded. None of the affected governments ordered any actions, but the combination of governmental displeasure and clear public disdain for Assange soon led a number of major Western corporations to withhold services from WikiLeaks. Amazon. com reclaimed rented server space that WikiLeaks had used, and

PayPal and MasterCard stopped processing donations made to WikiLeaks.

What soon followed might well be described as the first cyber battle between non-state actors. Supporters of WikiLeaks, loosely organized in a group under the name "Anonymous" (naturally), began a series of distributed denial-of-service (DDoS) attacks on the Web sites of major corporations that had taken an anti-WikiLeaks stand. (A DDoS attack uses many computers to flood an opponent's server with incoming communications, preventing legitimate efforts to connect to the server by sucking up bandwidth.) The Web site of the Swedish prosecuting authority (who is seeking Assange's extradition to Sweden to face criminal charges) was also hacked. Some of the coordination for the DDoS attacks was done through Facebook and Twitter. Meanwhile, other supporters created hundreds of mirror sites, replicating WikiLeaks content, so that it could not be effectively shut down. The hackers even adopted a military-style nomenclature, dubbing their efforts "Operation Payback."

When "Anonymous" attacked, the targets fought back. The major sites used defensive cyber protocols to oppose Anonymous. Most attacks were relatively unsuccessful—the announced attack on Amazon.com, for example, was abandoned shortly after it began because the assault did not succeed in preventing customers from accessing the Web site. Perhaps even more tellingly, someone (no group has, to this author's knowledge, publicly claimed credit) began an offensive cyber operation against Anonymous itself. Anonymous ran its operations through the Web site AnonOps.net, which was subject to DDoS counterattacks that took it offline for a number of hours. In short, a conflict readily recognizable as a battle between opposing forces was waged in cyberspace almost exclusively between non-state actors.

The Rise of Guerilla Cyberwar

The failure of Anonymous to effectively target corporate Web sites, and its relative vulnerability to counter-attack are likely only temporary circumstances. Both sides will learn from this battle and approach the next one with a greater degree of skill and a better perspective on how to achieve their ends. Indeed, Anonymous has made quite clear that it intends to continue to prosecute the cyberwar against, among others, the United States.

"It's a guerrilla cyberwar—that's what I call it," says Barrett Brown, 29, a self-described "propagandist" for Anonymous. "It's sort of an unconventional asymmetrical act of warfare that we're involved in, and we didn't necessarily start it. I mean, this fire has been burning." Or, consider the manifesto posted by Anonymous, declaring cyberspace independence from world governments: "I declare the global social space we are building together to be naturally independent of the tyrannies and injustices you seek to impose on us. You have no moral right to rule us nor do you possess any real methods of enforcement we have true reason to fear."

In advancing this agenda, the members of Anonymous look somewhat like the anarchists of the late 19th and early 20th centuries—albeit anarchists with a vastly greater network and far more ability to advance their agenda through individual action. But even more, they look like the non-state insurgents the U.S. has faced in Iraq and Afghanistan—small groups of non-state actors using asymmetric means of warfare to destabilize and disrupt existing political authority.

Implications for Cyberspace Conflict

The question is: How will governments respond? Are U.S. policymaking systems nimble enough to come to grips with the asymmetric empowerment of the net? More profoundly, has the growth of cyberspace begun a challenge to the hegemony of nation-states that has been the foundation for international relations since the Peace of Westphalia? Policymakers ought to learn at least three lessons about the state of conflict in cyberspace:

The Anonymous Collective

In some cases, online activists band together to form groups or collectives that exist only in cyberspace. One such collective named Anonymous is a self-styled group of online activists and hackers who helped construct mirror sites, then used Twitter services to call on other online activists to attack the sites of governments and companies deemed hostile to WikiLeaks. Anonymous and other groups engaged in hacktivism by attacking sites of companies and individuals who worked with governments to restrict access to WikiLeaks sites and funding.

In February 2010, Anonymous members allegedly hacked into a security firm investigating recent cyberattacks. FBI agents in the United States and police in other countries executed more than 40 arrest and seizure warrants on suspected members. In July 2011, the FBI—in cooperation with international law enforcement agencies—conducted another series of raids, arresting more than a dozen alleged members of the Anonymous hacking collective.

"Online Activism," Global Issues in
Context Online Collection, *2012.*

Asymmetric warfare is here to stay. The Anonymous challenge to large corporations and to governments worldwide is, in the end, inherent in the structure of the Internet. That structure allows individuals and small groups to wield power in cyberspace that is disproportionate to their numbers. Similarly, states can use electrons to do their fighting for them rather than sending armies into battle. States can also use non-state actors as proxies or mimic the activities of cyber insurgents to hide a government hand behind malicious activities. (It is suspected that China and Russia do precisely that.)

This description of the correlation of forces in cyberspace is, in many ways, congruent with similar analyses of the physical world. Terrorists enabled by asymmetric power (IEDs and box cutters) have likewise challenged traditional state authorities. And just as Americans must learn to deal with these kinetic insurgent challenges, so too must they respond to cyber insurgency.

Current capabilities of non-state actors are weak but improving. The current capabilities of organized non-state actors in cyberspace are relatively modest. While DDoS attacks can be a significant annoyance, they are not an existential threat. This state of affairs is unlikely to hold for long. As the recent Stuxnet computer virus demonstrates, significant real-world effects can already be achieved by sophisticated cyber actors. It is only a matter of time until less sophisticated non-state actors achieve the same capability.

Attribution is always a challenge. Determining the origin of an attack can be problematic. Sending a message from a digital device to a provider is akin to mailing a letter. The service provider acts as an electronic carrier that sends the message through routers and servers which deliver the message to the targeted computer. The "attacking" computers may have been hijacked and be under the control of a server in another country. An attacker may disguise its locations by circuitous routing or masking the message's source identification, similar to fudging a letter's return address and postmark. A cyber insurgent may strike several countries, multiple Internet service providers, and various telecommunications linkages, all subject to varying legal requirements and reporting standards, which makes tracing the source extremely difficult.

Overcoming these difficulties by technical means alone is a vexing problem—and an unnecessary one. The U.S. government should use *all* techniques in its arsenal to exploit the weaknesses of America's enemies.

Counterinsurgency vs. Cyberinsurgency

The problem of dealing with non-state actors like Anonymous resembles, in structure, the problem of dealing with a non-state insurgency on the ground in Iraq or Afghanistan, or with a state-sponsored proxy like the Iranian-backed Shia groups in Iraq. There are, of course, significant differences between the two domains. In the "kinetic" world, the goal of an insurgency is often the overthrow of an existing government. As the U.S. Army's Counterinsurgency Field Manual puts it: "Joint doctrine defines an *insurgency* as an organized movement aimed at the overthrow of a constituted government through the use of subversion and armed conflict. An insurgency is an organized, protracted politico—military struggle designed to weaken the control and legitimacy of an established government, occupying power, or other political authority while increasing insurgent control." WikiLeaks-like insurgents seem to have a different aim—"independence" from government. That independence is premised on weakening political authority over the cyber domain. While the goals may be different, conceptually the challenges pose many of the same problems—how to isolate fringe actors from the general populace and deny them support and refuge and, most of all, the freedom to attack at the time and place of their choosing.

In the past 10 years, the United States has devoted significant resources to the development of a counterinsurgency strategy for combating non-traditional warfare opponents on the ground. COIN requires a complex mix of offensive, defensive, and sustainment operations. In the context of a land-based operation, U.S. doctrine has had to consider a range of issues, including integrating military and civilian activity; collecting intelligence; building up host nation security services; maintaining essential services in-country; strengthening local governance; conducting offensive military operations; and fostering economic development. Each counterinsurgency campaign is different and the building blocks will vary, but these and other aspects will all play a critical role.

Elements of a Cyberinsurgency Strategy

The U.S. government has yet to develop an equivalent COIN strategy for cyberspace. The American strategy must be much more expansive than treating cyber threats as primarily a technical challenge. Concepts that might find their way into a cyber insurgency approach to battling bad actors online include:

Collecting Intelligence. Dealing with cyber insurgents requires human intelligence (HUMINT) on the operation of non-state actors in cyberspace. Rather than concentrating on technical intelligence, "human intelligence" focuses on information collected by human sources (such as through conversations and interrogations). HUMINT can provide all kinds of information on the cyber insurgents, not only the technical means of attack, but motivations, relationships, and finances—identifying weaknesses and vulnerabilities in their network that might not be available from merely deconstructing malicious software or looking through the files of an Internet service provider. Indeed, HUMINT and related intelligence tools may be the only means to positively attribute the source of an attack—one of the most critical tasks in combating cyber insurgents. Current U.S. strategies give short shrift to the critical role of a more comprehensive intelligence effort for cybersecurity. President Obama's National Security Strategy, for example, defines the mission of "securing cyberspace" exclusively in terms of designing "more secure technology" and investing in "cutting-edge research and development." The strategy includes no discussion of the role of intelligence in cybersecurity.

Likewise, when Deputy Secretary of Defense William Lynn outlined the five pillars of the Department of Defense's cyber strategy, he emphasized the technical aspects of the threat and neglected to address the role of intelligence. Intelligence, however, could be crucial to identifying how to weaken the threat other than merely shutting down its servers. Good "ground" intelligence could be the precursor to other means at affecting the enemy (means that might range from a "naming and shaming" campaign to an assault on his financial assets to a direct attack).

Integrating Government and Civilian Action. As in the kinetic world, much of the U.S. effort will require coordination between military and civilian government assets. In cyberspace, the situation has the added layer of complexity posed by the need to coordinate with private-sector actors. President Obama's National Security Strategy rightly emphasizes the importance of public-private partnerships: "Neither government nor the private sector nor the individual citizen," the strategy notes, "can meet this challenge alone."

When coordinated action is done well, it can have a demonstrative impact. In one recent case, the FBI worked with companies that had been identified as being infected with a "botnet" program called Coreflood, malicious software that infects Microsoft Windows-based computers and is designed to steal usernames, passwords, and financial information. According to a court affidavit filed in the case: In one example, the chief information security officer of a hospital healthcare network reported that, after being notified of the Coreflood infection, a preliminary investigation revealed that approximately 2,000 of the hospital's 14,000 computers were infected by Coreflood. Because Coreflood had stopped running on the infected computers, the hospital was able to focus on investigating and repairing the damage instead of undertaking emergency efforts to stop the loss of data from the infected computers.

The Coreflood case and cooperative public-private activities, such as the U.S. Computer Emergency Readiness Team (US-CERT) program, demonstrate that despite the myriad legal, cultural, and bureaucratic obstacles, effective cooperation is possible.

For a cyber insurgency strategy to be effective, it is critical that the U.S. develop mechanisms for ensuring that "successes" and "best practices" are translated into a suitable doctrine and become part of the professional development of private-sector and public-sector leaders. Among other needs will be demands for education, training, and experience that qualify public and private actors to be real cyber leaders. A doctrine that addresses public-private cooperation must be a centerpiece of that strategy. No adequate effort to address this shortfall is currently underway.

Building Host Nation Cybersecurity. Strengthening the capacity of friends and allies for network security and resilience has to be an essential part of counter-cyberinsurgency. The more that nations with common purpose and values work together, the more that can be done to shrink the cyberspace available to cyber insurgents. In the case of the recent Coreflood investigation, for example, in response to a request by the U.S. for assistance from Estonia under the Mutual Legal Assistance Treaty between the two countries, law enforcement authorities there advised the FBI of the seizure of several additional computer servers believed to be "predecessors" to Coreflood command-and-control servers in the United States. Estonia has undertaken some of the most innovative efforts to protect its nation's cyber-infrastructure and deal with cyber crimes and cyber attacks. Estonia counts as a first-class cyber ally. The U.S. could use many more such allies. Washington needs to encourage other nations to take similar steps to enhance their capabilities. This might be done through innovative assistance programs, such as the proposed Security for Freedom Fund (intended to assist other countries with their development of homeland security systems), or by cooperative agreements that model the U.S. SAFETY Act (which provides liability protection to companies that develop innovative new technologies).

The foregoing is just a start—other questions of resilience and offensive operations will also need to be addressed. These kinds of initiatives reflect how all the nation's resources should be employed in the cyber war. To win the battle for cyberspace, cyber strategy must become much more multifaceted.

The U.S. can, as it did in Iraq, wait until the need for such a strategy is brought home by failures on the ground. Or, the U.S. can, more wisely, see the WikiLeaks war as a wake-up call and begin the necessary doctrinal thinking now.

> *"A regulatory program would likely become highly rigid in practice and thus counterproductive to effective cybersecurity."*

More Government Regulation Would Impede Innovation and Cybersecurity

Tom Ridge

Tom Ridge is the former secretary of the Department of Homeland Security and the chairman of the National Security Task Force of the US Chamber of Commerce. In the following viewpoint, he acknowledges that improving cybersecurity is essential to US businesses and infrastructure but expresses opposition to recent legislative proposals that would impose rigid regulations on US businesses. Ridge argues that a regulatory program would be counterproductive to cybersecurity by shifting focus from security to compliance and hampering the agility and innovation of companies to respond to a myriad of cyberthreats. Instead, Ridge recommends that legislative efforts should focus on enhancing the collaboration between industry and government partners and providing businesses with timely information on emerging cyberthreats.

Tom Ridge, "Securing America's Future: The Cybersecurity Act of 2012," Testimony for the US Senate Committee on Homeland Security and Governmental Affairs, February 16, 2012.

As you read, consider the following questions:

1. According to Ridge's description, what does the Homeland Security Presidential Directive No. 7 do?
2. How does Ridge describe the goal of the Cybersecurity Act of 2012?
3. What is the Small Biz Cyber Planner, according to Ridge?

The business community recognizes the opportunities and challenges inherent in our interconnected world. The Internet has transformed the global economy and connected people in new and exciting ways. It helps drive progress in almost every aspect of our lives. Businesses of all sizes are increasingly dependent on the Internet for their day-to-day operations. Cyber technologies help businesses achieve great efficiencies, and they help run our vital infrastructures—from the shop floor to energy production to banking and much more.

Unfortunately, bad actors—such as organized criminals, "hacktivists," and foreign governments—have taken advantage of a cyber environment that is more open and welcoming than secure. The Chamber [of Commerce] and members of its National Security Task Force are keenly aware of cyber threats to American businesses and the nation. The Director of National Intelligence, James Clapper, recently testified about the scope and nature of cybersecurity incidents as well as the range of actors and targets. His insights help inform our discussion.

An essential question facing policymakers is: How do we continue to develop public policies that improve economic and national security? The Chamber believes there is a growing consensus about measures that can help counter illicit cyber intruders and earn broad bipartisan support, which I will touch on further in my remarks. Over the past few years, the Chamber has stated that it will support legislation, such as an information-sharing bill, that is carefully targeted toward effectively addressing the complex cyber threats that businesses are experiencing.

The Private Sector Strives to Enhance Its Security

Businesses strive to stay a step ahead of cybercriminals and protect potentially sensitive consumer and business information by employing sound risk-management principles. Industry has been taking robust and proactive steps for many years to protect and make their information networks more resilient.

The protection of U.S. critical infrastructure has a lengthy history. Issued in 1998, Presidential Decision Directive No. 63 (PDD-63) helped spur the protection of critical infrastructure and cybersecurity and as well helped launch the formation of Information Sharing and Analysis Centers (ISACs) across the private sector. In 2003, Homeland Security Presidential Directive No. 7 (HSPD-7) updated the policy of the United States and the roles and responsibilities of various agencies related to critical infrastructure identification, prioritization, and protection.

Jumping forward a few years, 2006 witnessed the creation of the National Infrastructure Protection Plan (NIPP) and the Critical Infrastructure Protection Advisory [Council (CIPAC)]. The NIPP resulted in the establishment of Sector Coordinating Councils and Government Coordinating Councils to work together on furthering the protection and resilience of the critical infrastructure community under the authorities of CIPAC. The NIPP was revised in 2009 to reflect an evolution of the process, including expanded integration of all-hazard and similarly important principles.

Cybersecurity Is Essential to Risk Reduction

Businesses are heavily focused on guarding their operations from interruption, preventing the loss of capital or intellectual property, and protecting public safety. They devote considerable resources toward maintaining their operations in the wake of a natural hazard or man-made threat, such as a cyberattack.

Business owners and operators understand it is imperative that information infrastructure be well protected and resilient.

Cybersecurity is viewed as an essential aspect of risk reduction, just like risk management related to physical threats. Industry activities have included development of guides, road maps, and standards to improve security, operational safety, and reliability. Sector leaders undertake exercises, which the Chamber encourages, to assess and improve facility and system capabilities. In sum, private-sector owners and operators routinely strive to strengthen the security of their cyber systems and identify and mitigate any network vulnerability.

The businesses community already complies with multiple information security rules. Among the regulatory requirements impacting businesses of all sizes are the Chemical Facilities Anti-Terrorism Standards (CFATS), the Federal Energy Regulatory Commission-North American Reliability Corporation Critical Information Protection (FERC-NERC CIP) standards, the Gramm-Leach-Bliley Act (GLBA), the Health Insurance Portability and Accountability Act (HIPAA), and the Sarbanes-Oxley (SOX) Act. Instead of adding to the regulatory burden, Congress should work to reduce the fragmented and often conflicting burdens that these different rules and bureaucracies place on industry.

More Regulation Would Impede Cybersecurity

The Cybersecurity Act of 2012 would authorize DHS to establish a regime for regulating the assets or systems of vital parts of the American economy. Given the discretion that government officials would have in designating "covered" critical infrastructure (CCI), the likelihood for DHS to regulate entities in many American communities is considerable. Instead of taking this less optimal route, the Chamber believes that policymakers should utilize and improve upon the sector-based risk assessments already being conducted by DHS.

Advocates of a regulatory CCI program argue, "We propose a 'light-touch' approach to regulation." However, the Chamber is concerned not only with the concept but with how it would be implemented. During the implementation phase of a regulatory CCI program, it would likely shift from being standards- and risk-based and flexible in concept to being overly prescriptive in practice.

A regulatory program would likely become highly rigid in practice and thus counterproductive to effective cybersecurity—due in large part to a shift in businesses' focus from security to compliance. Equally concerning, federal mandates could compromise security. By homogenizing security, our online adversaries would quickly learn to circumvent a company's protections and those of similarly situated companies.

It is not unreasonable to think that Congress, with the myriad issues on its plate, would find it challenging to maintain a level of vigilance necessary to ensure that the regulatory CCI program does not become prescriptive and detrimental to security. Contrary to some news headlines, the private sector routinely thwarts cyberattacks against its networks because it is fast and nimble in its response and recovery efforts. The Chamber is deeply concerned that a new regulatory regime would box in our critical infrastructures, hampering the freedom, agility, and innovation needed to deflect or defeat adversaries who are often quite amply resourced.

In addition to a regulatory CCI program, the Chamber is concerned about proposals that call on the owners and operators of CCI to develop risk mitigation plans that would be evaluated by a third-party auditor. Complying with third-party assessments would be costly and time consuming, particularly for small businesses. Most businesses already have processes in place for assessing and improving the strength of their networks, so added mandates are unnecessary if not misguided. Many in the business community are concerned that the release of proprietary information to third parties could actually create new security risks.

Also, the Chamber opposes any proposal requiring CCI to report any significant cyber incident to DHS or another government body. Information sharing is a two-way street, but this incredibly broad reporting threshold would be unworkable in practice and, perhaps, unhelpful because of data overload. From a fairness standpoint, legislative proposals lack any comparable requirement that government entities share threat information with CCI.

Policy Makers Should Advance Collaborative Risk Assessments

Over the past year, the Chamber has developed and worked with other industry organizations on cybersecurity proposals that offer positive and cooperative approaches to increasing U.S. information security and resilience.

The Chamber believes that policymakers should leverage and improve upon the sector-based risk assessments already being conducted by DHS or sector-specific agencies and industry under the existing NIPP. A key premise behind advocating collaborative sector-based risk assessments is to help answer a question that policymakers frequently ask: How are we doing on cybersecurity? Unfortunately, this question leads some to want to regulate the businesses community in prescriptive and unhelpful ways.

The Chamber has written a proposal advocating that DHS and industry sectors routinely produce a sector or subsector risk assessment that paints a picture of the strengths and vulnerabilities of the sector's cyber preparedness and resilience against a significant disruption, such as a cyberattack or a natural hazard. In contrast, the bill seems to use sector assessments as a springboard to increased regulation, rather than toward greater collaboration. Policymakers should ensure that the private sector and the federal government have done nearly everything they can within the public-private partnership framework to enhance U.S. cybersecurity before making a leap to an uncertain regulatory program.

The Economic Threat of Cybercrime

The warnings of our vulnerability to a major cyber attack come from all directions and countless experts, and are underscored by the intrusions that have already occurred. Earlier this month [February 2012], FBI Director Robert Mueller warned that the cyber threat will soon equal or surpass the threat from terrorism. He argued that we should be addressing the cyber threat with the same intensity we have applied to the terrorist threat.

Director of National Intelligence James Clapper made the point even more strongly, describing the cyber threat as a "profound threat to this country, to its future, its economy and its very being."

Last November, the director of the Defense Advanced Research Projects Agency or DARPA warned that malicious cyber attacks threaten a growing number of the systems we interact with daily—like the power grid, water treatment plants, and key financial systems.

Similarly, General Keith Alexander, commander of U.S. Cyber Command and director of the National Security Agency, warned that the cyber vulnerabilities we face are extraordinary and characterized by "a disturbing trend, from exploitation to disruption to destruction."

These statements are just the latest in a chorus of warnings from current and former officials. The threat is not just to our national security, but also to our economic well-being.

Susan M. Collins, "Securing America's
Future: The Cybersecurity Act of 2012,"
US Committee on Homeland Security and
Governmental Affairs, February 12, 2012.

The U.S. Government Should Boost Public Awareness

For several years, the Chamber has partnered with DHS and other agencies to increase businesses' knowledge of cybersecurity from an enterprise risk-management perspective. The Chamber has also promoted *Stop. Think. Connect.*, a public-private education and awareness campaign to help people stay safer and more secure online. But more needs to be done. We recommend heeding the example of government and industry mobilization in 2009 to halt the spread of the H1N1 flu virus. Simple and effective resources were made available to households, businesses, and schools across the country to mitigate the impact of the outbreak.

This collaborative effort could serve as a model for stemming much of the nefarious and comparatively unsophisticated activity seen online, freeing up limited human and capital resources to focus on more advanced and persistent threats. The Chamber recently partnered with the Federal Communications Commission (FCC) to unveil the FCC's new Small Biz Cyber Planner, a free online tool to help small businesses protect themselves from cybersecurity threats and make the price of attacks steep for their digital adversaries.

Congress Should Enact a Meaningful Information-Sharing Bill

Cybersecurity is a significant economic and national security issue that the Chamber takes very seriously. We believe that the right path forward is for the public and private sectors to work together to solve challenges, to share information between network managers, and foster investment and innovation in cybersecurity technologies. The optimal way forward will not be found in layering additional regulations on the business community. New compliance mandates would drive up costs and misallocate business resources without necessarily increasing security.

Critical infrastructure owners and operators devote significant resources toward protecting and making resilient their information systems because it is in their overwhelming interest to do so. The Chamber urges Congress to support efforts that genuinely enhance collaboration between industry and government partners.

In addition, the Chamber supports information-sharing legislation that would address the need of businesses to receive timely and actionable information from government analysts to protect their enterprises by improving detection, prevention, mitigation, and response through enhanced situational awareness. The legislation should build on the recent defense industrial base (DIB) pilot project as a potential model for demonstrating how government cyber threat intelligence can be shared with the private sector in an operationally usable manner.

Businesses need certainty that threat information voluntarily shared with the government would be exempt from public disclosure and prohibited from use by officials in regulatory matters. Legislation needs to provide legal protection for companies that guard their own networks in good faith or disclose cyber threat information with appropriate entities, such as ISACs.

> *"Just as the US was the first to use the atomic bomb . . . it is . . . taking the lead in a new global arms race in cyber warfare and drone technology."*

The United States Should Engage in Cyberwarfare Treaty Talks

Alice Slater

Alice Slater is the New York director of the Nuclear Age Peace Foundation. In the following viewpoint, she questions the opposition of US officials to consider negotiations on a treaty limiting cyberwarfare between countries and drone technology. Slater accuses the United States of engaging in a new arms race with Russia and China, which could have devastating consequences for the world. Slater charges that the scientists involved in such research are irresponsible, comparing the new global arms race to the nuclear arms race. She urges the United States to reconsider its stance and set a good example for world peace.

As you read, consider the following questions:

1. In what year did India perform its first nuclear test, according to Slater?

2. How many nuclear weapons does Slater estimate are mounted on missiles poised to fire against Russian missiles?
3. According to Slater, how much money will fund the "stockpile stewardship" program for the next ten years?

In 2000, I traveled to India, invited to speak at the organizing meeting of the Indian Coalition for Nuclear Disarmament and Peace. About 600 organizations, including some 80 from Pakistan gathered in New Delhi to strategize for nuclear disarmament. India had quietly acquired the bomb and performed one nuclear test at Pokhran in 1974 but it was in 1998 that all hell broke out, with India exploding five underground tests, swiftly followed by six in Pakistan.

The trigger for this outbreak of nuclear testing in Asia was the refusal of the US [president Bill] Clinton Administration, under the pressure of the US nuclear weapons scientists, to negotiate a Comprehensive Test Ban Treaty [CTBT] that precluded laboratory testing and "sub-critical" tests, where plutonium could be blown up underground with chemicals without causing a chain reaction—hence defined as a non-nuclear test by the US and the nuclear club. India warned the nuclear powers at the Commission on Disarmament (CD) where the CTBT was being negotiated, that it opposed the CTBT because it contained discriminatory "loopholes . . . exploited by some countries to continue their testing activity, using more sophisticated and advanced techniques," and it would never agree to consensus on the treaty unless the ability to continue high-tech laboratory testing and computer-driven nuclear experiments was foreclosed.

In an unprecedented move of colonial hubris, Australia, led by Ambassador Richard Butler, brought the treaty to the UN for approval over India's objections, the first time in the history of that body that the UN General Assembly was asked to endorse a treaty that had not received consensus to go forward in the negotiating body at the CD. I spoke to Ambassador Butler at a

UN reception where the wine was flowing a bit liberally. I asked him what he was going to do about India's objection. He informed me that he had been visiting with Clinton's National Security Advisor in Washington, Sandy Berger, and Berger said, "We're going to screw India! We're going to screw India!", repeated twice by Butler, for emphasis. Unsurprisingly, India and Pakistan soon tested overtly, not wanting to be left behind in the technology race for new improved nuclear weapons which was characterized blasphemously by the US in biblical terms, as its "stockpile stewardship" program to protect the "safety and reliability" of the arsenal.

The Safety of the US Nuclear Arsenal

As for the "safety and reliability" of the nuclear arsenal, in the late 1980s, during the heady days of *perestroika* and *glasnost*, when there was talk of a nuclear testing moratorium, initially instituted in the Soviet Union after coal miners and other activists marched and protested the enormous health threats from Russian testing in Kazakhstan, a debate in Congress resulted in an annotated Congressional record indicating that since 1950 there were 32 airplane crashes carrying nuclear weapons and not one of them ever went off! Two spewed some plutonium around Palomares, Spain and Thule, Greenland that had to be "cleaned up", but there was no catastrophic nuclear explosion. There are still some bombs unaccounted for including an airplane still missing which crashed off the coast of Georgia. How much more "safer and reliable" would the weapons have to be?

Fortunately, General Lee Butler, taking command of the nuclear arsenal stopped the insanity in 1992 and ruled that the planes carrying nuclear weapons would be grounded instead of being in the air 24/7 keeping us "safe" and "deterring" the Soviet Union. What could they have been thinking? Sadly, there has been no corresponding move to ratchet down the lunacy that endangers our planet at every moment from some 1,500 deployed nuclear weapons mounted on missiles poised to fire against Russian missiles, similarly cocked, in minutes.

Even before "stockpile stewardship," I remember attending a meeting with the mad scientists at Los Alamos National Laboratory, home of Dr. Strangelove, and sitting in a circle to discuss the aftermath of nuclear policy in the shadow of the crumbled wall in Berlin. The scientists were earnestly discussing the need for AGEX (Above Ground Experiments), to keep their nuclear mind-muscles alive and limber, which eventually morphed into the diabolically named "stockpile stewardship" program. Today, that misbegotten program is funded to the tune of $84 billion over the next ten years, with another $100 billion budgeted for new "delivery" systems—missiles, submarine, airplanes—as if the Cold War had never ended!

At the Delhi conference, Dr. Amulya Reddy, a nuclear physicist gave an electrifying talk on the responsibility of science and its moral failures, explaining how shocked he was to find documents describing how the German scientists carefully calculated, with extraordinary accuracy and scientific precision, the amount of poison gas required per person to kill the Jews who were routinely marched to the Nazi "showers" in the concentration camps. And at a workshop on the role of science, there was an extraordinary conversation with Indian and Pakistani scientists who pondered whether scientists have lost their moral compass because the system of higher education produced the growth of the scientific institute, isolating scientists from the arts and humanities. They examined whether these separated tracks of learning, denying scientists the opportunity to intermingle with colleagues engaged in those issues, while narrowly concentrating on their scientific disciplines, had stunted their intellectual and moral growth and led them to forget their humanity.

US Scientists Are Forging a New Arms Race

Now scientists are pushing whatever boundaries might have existed to open a whole new avenue of terror and danger for the world. In a profound disregard for the consequences of their actions, US scientists are enabling a new arms race with Russia and China as the military-industrial-academic-Congressional complex plants US missiles in Eastern Europe and beefs up military bases in the Pacific. This despite efforts by Russia and China to forestall this new arms race by calling for a treaty to ban weapons in space, supported by every nation in the world except the US which blocks any forward progress for negotiations.

The US has recently admitted to cyber warfare, targeting uranium enrichment equipment in Iran with a killer virus to set back the Iranian program to build their own bomb in the basement, while at home, we are talking of massive subsidies to the uranium enrichment factory in Paducah, Kentucky. It is hard to believe how screwy this new venture into cyber warfare is in terms of providing security to the "homeland." After all, cyber terror is not nuclear warfare. Any country, or even scores of various groups of individuals, can master the technology undetected, and wreak catastrophic havoc on the myriads of civilian computer-dependent systems, local, national, and global. Similarly, the recent expansion of drone warfare, assassinating innocent civilians together with suspected "terrorists" in eight countries, at last count, with the President of the US acting as judge, jury and executioner, is the application of misbegotten science in a recipe for endless illegal war. Just as the US was the first to use the atomic bomb, opening the door to the disturbing and uncontrollable nuclear proliferation we witness today, it is again opening the door, taking the lead in a new global arms race in cyber warfare and drone technology. Despite Russia's suggestion that there be a treaty against cyber war, the US is resisting negotiations, indicating their continued arrogance and disregard of what must be manifestly apparent to any rational thinking person. There can be no reasonable expectation that scientists can keep the dark fruits of their lethal discoveries from proliferating around the world. It is just so 20th century, hierarchical and left-brained to imagine that there will not be others to follow their evil example, or that they can somehow control an outbreak of the same destructive technology to others who may not wish them well.

Holding the Planet Hostage

Can there be any doubt that scientists driving US policy are out of touch with reality? Officials talk about "risk assessment" as though the dreadful disastrous events at Chernobyl and Fukushima are capable of being weighed on a scale of risks and benefits. Scientists are constantly refining their nuclear weapons and designing new threats to the fate of the Earth. After the horrendous devastation in Hiroshima and Nagasaki, surely everyone with half a brain knows these catastrophic bombs are completely unusable and yet we're pouring all these billions of dollars into perpetuating the weapons labs, as hunger and homelessness increase in the US and our infrastructure is crumbling. The high priests of Science are not including the Earth in their calculations and the enormous havoc they are wreaking on our air, water, soil, our biosphere. They're thinking with the wrong half of their brains—without integrating the intuitive part of thinking that would curb their aggressive tendencies which engender such deadly, irreversible possibilities. They are engaged in creating the worst possible inventions with a Pandora's box of lethal consequences that may plague the earth for eternity. Still, they continue on. Scientists are holding our planet hostage while they tinker in their laboratories without regard to the risks they are creating for the very future of life on Earth.

Periodical and Internet Sources Bibliography

The following articles have been selected to supplement the diverse views presented in this chapter.

Dave Aitel	"The Cybersecurity Act of 2012: Are We Smarter than a Fifth Grader?," *Huffington Post*, August 3, 2012. www.huffingtonpost.com.
David Inserra	"Cybersecurity Legislation Should Be Done Well or Not at All," *The Foundry*, July 25, 2012. blog.heritage.org.
Mark M. Jaycox	"The Cybersecurity Act Was a Surveillance Bill in Disguise," *The Guardian*, August 2, 2012. www .guardian.co.uk.
Erik Kain	"Does the Cybersecurity Act of 2012 Mark the Beginning of the War on Cyber-Terrorism?," *Forbes .com*, February 22, 2012. www .forbes.com.
Adam Levin	"The Profound Failure of Congress on Cyber Security (and Why You Should Care)," *Huffington Post*, August 9, 2012. www.huffington post.com.
John Naughton	"Stuxnet: The Worm That Turned Obama into a Hypocrite," *The Guardian*, June 9, 2012. www .guardian.co.uk.
Paul Rosenzweig	"Cybersecurity Act of 2012: Revised Cyber Bill Still Has Problems," Heritage Foundation, July 23, 2012. www.heritage.org.
Ginny Sloan	"New Cybersecurity Bill Provides Significantly Improved Privacy Safeguards," *Huffington Post*, July 23, 2012. www.huffingtonpost .com.
Wall Street Journal	"No Cybersecurity Executive Order, Please," September 13, 2012. online.wsj.com.

For Further Discussion

Chapter 1

1. What are the most effective ways to protect US cybersecurity? Read all of the viewpoints in the chapter to learn about different perspectives on the issue. Which viewpoint do you feel makes the best argument? Why?

2. Sue Marquette Poremba contends that ethical hackers could be useful when it comes to protecting cybersecurity. In their viewpoint, Conrad Constantine and Dominique Karg argue that the concept of ethical hacking is a myth. After reading both perspectives, do you think ethical hacking can make a significant difference when it comes to combating hacking?

Chapter 2

1. Is hacktivism an ethical means of social protest or just an effective way for radicals and terrorists to disrupt computer networks and threaten a nation's national security? Read viewpoints by Graham Armstrong and Phil Elmore to illuminate the issue.

2. Free speech on the Internet is a hotly debated topic. James Ball believes that hacktivists work to protect civil liberties and free expression. Elinor Mills maintains that many hacktivists are hypocrites, because they shut down the websites of political and social opponents and deny speech that they do not like. What is your opinion on the issue? What is the best way to protect free expression and civil liberties on the Internet?

Chapter 3

1. After reading all of the viewpoints in the chapter, which perspective do you believe best fits your own view of WikiLeaks? What do you think that the legacy of WikiLeaks will be?

2. Marc A. Thiessen argues that WikiLeaks is a dire threat to US national security. John B. Judis asserts that WikiLeaks may actually improve US foreign policy in the long run. Which author makes the more persuasive argument?

Chapter 4

1. How should nations respond to cyberattacks? The US Department of Defense states that the United States has the right to respond with a military attack. Benjamin H. Friedman and Christopher Preble argue that such an exaggerated response is dangerous. Which viewpoint do you agree with and why?

2. Tom Ridge argues that adding regulations would impede innovation from the private sector and make corporations and businesses more vulnerable to cyberattacks. Do you support cyberlegislation to strengthen US cyberdefenses? Why or why not?

Organizations to Contact

The editors have compiled the following list of organizations concerned with the issues debated in this book. The descriptions are derived from materials provided by the organizations. All have publications or information available for interested readers. The list was compiled on the date of publication of the present volume; names, addresses, phone and fax numbers, and email and Internet addresses may change. Be aware that many organizations take several weeks or longer to respond to inquiries, so allow as much time as possible.

Central Intelligence Agency (CIA)
Office of Public Affairs
Washington, DC 20505
(703) 482-0623 • fax: (703) 482-1739
website: www.cia.gov

Established in 1947, the CIA is the civilian intelligence agency of the US government. It is responsible for gathering intelligence on foreign governments and terrorist organizations and provides national security assessments to US policy makers. The CIA's intelligence-gathering activities range from assessing emerging and existing threats to the US government to monitoring and analyzing correspondence and Internet communications, implementing tactical operations in foreign countries, developing and managing intelligence assets, launching counterterrorism efforts, and dealing with threats to US computer systems. The CIA website offers a featured story archive, recent press releases and statements, speeches and testimony by CIA officials, and a page for kids to learn about CIA initiatives.

Computer Security Institute (CSI)
350 Hudson Street, Suite 300
New York, NY 10014

email: csi@ubm.com
website: gocsi.com

CSI is an educational membership organization made up of security professionals interested in staying at the forefront of cybersecurity trends, technology, and strategies. CSI members aid companies and organizations in upgrading and maintaining a high level of cybersecurity, focusing on three core areas: educating employers about emerging cyberthreats, valuable resources, and useful tools and strategies; providing a community for employers and employees to exchange ideas and stay abreast of cybersecurity trends, including CSI conferences, helpful forums, and informative blogs; and offering access to a range of current research on cybersecurity topics on the CSI website. Also available on the CSI website are webinars, extensive training courses, and publications including its annual *CSI Computer Crime and Security Survey* and the *Computer Security Alert*.

Electronic Frontier Foundation (EFF)
454 Shotwell Street
San Francisco, CA 94110
(415) 436-9333 • fax: (415) 436-9993
email: info@eff.org
website: www.eff.org

EFF was established in 1990 to protect the rights of individuals and businesses in cyberspace from government interference and persecution. To that end, the EFF takes on legal cases to set precedent on the issue of Internet freedom and confirm the rights of individuals and business in cyberspace. Over the years, the EFF has come to address emerging threats to Internet freedom from industry, especially in the area of copyright law. Another role of the EFF is the fight for privacy on the Internet, particularly in situations where governments monitor Internet communications in the interest of national security. The EFF informs hackers, whistleblowers, and anyone on the Internet of their rights under the law and offers assistance to anyone under government suspicion or surveillance. The organization's website has a range of information on topical issues, including hacking, privacy, innovation, copyright law, and bloggers' rights. It also hosts a blog that covers recent events and research, breaking news, upcoming EFF initiatives and legal cases, and relevant policies all over the world.

Federal Bureau of Investigation (FBI)

935 Pennsylvania Avenue NW
Washington, DC 20535
(202) 324-3000
website: www.fbi.gov

The FBI is the US law enforcement agency with the mission "to protect and defend the United States against terrorist and foreign intelligence threats, to uphold and enforce the criminal laws of the United States, and to provide leadership and criminal justice services to federal, state, municipal, and international agencies and partners." One of its central responsibilities is to protect the United States against cyber-based attacks and high-technology crimes, such as major cyberfraud and identity theft. The FBI website lists the top cybercriminals, outlines the agency's key priorities, introduces recent initiatives and cases, and offers educational materials on how to protect one's privacy in cyberspace. The website also allows users to sign up for the National Cyber Awareness System feeds, which alerts subscribers to current scams, viruses, and other threats to their cybersecurity.

Information Systems Security Association (ISSA)

9220 SW Barbur Blvd. #119-333
Portland, OR 97219
(866) 349-5818 • fax: (206) 299-3366
website: www.issa.org

ISSA is a nonprofit international organization of information security professionals devoted to providing informative educational resources and training materials for its members. ISSA's central goal is to "promote management practices that will ensure the confidentiality, integrity, and availability of information resources" and "facilitate interaction and education to create a more successful environment for global information systems security and for the professionals involved." ISSA organizes international conferences, seminars, and local chapter meetings to provide hands-on training and education in the latest methods and technology; coordinates ISSA connect, a networking forum that allows members to exchange ideas; and publishes a monthly periodical, the *ISSA Journal*, as well as frequent e-newsletters.

National Counterterrorism Center (NCTC)
Office of the Director of National Intelligence
Washington, DC 20511
(703) 733-8600
website: www.nctc.gov

An agency of the Office of the Director of National Intelligence (DNI), the NCTC analyzes emerging and existing threats to the safety of the United States, disseminates relevant intelligence with other government agencies and partners, develops operational strategies, and marshals the resources of the national government to address those threats effectively. The NCTC also advises the DNI on intelligence analysis and operations relating to counterterrorism and serves as the central resource for all information on counterterrorism activities and intelligence. The NCTC website has press releases, interviews, speeches and testimony from NCTC officials as well as published reports, fact sheets, and the legislation that established the center. There is also a NCTC kids page, which offers an introduction to the NCTC and its activities for young children.

National Cyber Security Division (NCSD)
12th and C Street SW
Washington, DC 20024

(202) 282-8000

website: http://www.dhs.gov/national-cyber-security
-division

The NCSD is a division of the Department of Homeland Security (DHS) that focuses on protecting US national security in cyberspace. The NCSD coordinates public, private, and international entities to secure US assets; monitors and analyzes cyberthreats; and maintains the National Cyber Alert System, which informs public and private entities of potential cyberattacks. NCSD maintains the US-CERT system, which recognizes threats and coordinating response strategies. It also coordinates the Cyber Storm, an international cybersecurity exercise to test the response to a catastrophic cyberattack.

National Security Agency/Central Security Service (NSA/CSS)

9800 Savage Road

Fort Meade, MD 20755

(301) 688-6524 • fax: (301) 688-6198

email: nsapao@nsa.gov

website: www.nsa.gov

The NSA/CSS is a partnership between two of the premier US national security organizations: The NSA offers timely foreign policy analysis for US political and military leaders; and the CSS provides cryptological knowledge and assistance and develops policies for the national-security community. One of the organization's key missions is Information Assurance, a strategy to prevent foreign countries and individual hackers from gaining access to classified national security information and to shore up vulnerabilities in US cybersecurity. The NSA/CSS website offers access to recent press releases and breaking news, transcripts of speeches and testimony of NSA/CSS staff, and *Next Wave*, an agency journal that publishes in-depth articles, commentary, and research.

US Department of Homeland Security (DHS)
12th and C Street SW
Washington, DC 20024
(202) 282-8000
website: www.dhs.gov

The DHS is tasked with protecting the United States from terrorist attacks and other threats. Established after the terrorist attacks of September 11, 2001, the DHS aims to reduce the vulnerability of US infrastructure and installations, government officials, and major events, to attacks of any kind; enforce and administer immigration laws to better control who is traveling in and out of the country; coordinate and administer the national response to terrorist attacks and be a key player in recovery and rebuilding efforts; and to safeguard and secure cyberspace by assessing cyberthreats and coordinating a counterattack. The DHS works closely with other government agencies and relevant partners to protect the nation's cybersecurity. The DHS website allows access to a number of informative resources, including fact sheets, breaking news, press releases, speeches and testimony of DHS officials, video, and other publications on topics of interest.

US Secret Service
245 Murray Drive, Building 410
Washington, DC 20223
(202) 406-5708
email: www.secretservice.gov

The US Secret Service is the federal law enforcement agency tasked with protecting national and foreign leaders and carrying out major investigations into crimes such as counterfeiting. It is also authorized to establish a network of Electronic Crimes Task Forces (ECTFs), which coordinate the activities of federal, state, and local law enforcement, the private sector, researchers and academia, and other legal professionals on the issue of electronic crimes. These crimes include unauthorized access to protected computer networks, data theft, distributed denial-of-service attacks, and malware distribution meant for commercial or personal gain. ECTFs focus on cybercrimes launched for financial gain, not national security. The Secret Service website offers information on recent investigations, breaking news, and a photo gallery of the agency in action.

Bibliography of Books

Charles Beckett with James Ball — *WikiLeaks: News in the Networked Era.* Cambridge, MA: Polity, 2012.

Joel Brenner — *America the Vulnerable: Inside the New Threat Matrix of Digital Espionage, Crime, and Warfare.* New York: Penguin, 2011.

Susan W. Brenner — *Cybercrime: Criminal Threats from Cyberspace.* Santa Barbara, CA: Praeger, 2010.

Susan W. Brenner — *Cybercrime and the Law: Challenges, Issues, and Outcomes.* Boston: Northeastern University Press, 2012.

Jeffrey Carr — *Inside Cyber Warfare.* Sebastopol, CA: O'Reilly Media, 2010.

Raoul Chiesa, Stefania Ducci, and Silvio Ciappi — *Profiling Hackers: The Science of Criminal Profiling as Applied to the World of Hacking.* Boca Raton, FL: Auerbach, 2009.

Jonathan Clough — *Principles of Cybercrime.* New York: Cambridge University Press, 2012.

Christopher Coker — *Warrior Geeks: How 21st-Century Technology Is Changing the Way We Fight and Think About War.* New York: Columbia University Press, 2012.

E. Gabriella Coleman — *Coding Freedom: The Ethics and Aesthetics of Hacking*. Princeton, NJ: Princeton University Press, 2012.

Heather Harrison Dinniss — *Cyber Warfare and the Laws of War*. New York: Cambridge University Press, 2012.

John David Ebert — *The New Media Invasion: Digital Technologies and the World They Unmake*. Jefferson, NC: McFarland, 2011.

Jon Erickson — *Hacking: The Art of Exploitation*, second ed. San Francisco: No Starch, 2008.

Andrew Fowler — *The Most Dangerous Man in the World: The Explosive True Story of Julian Assange and the Lies, Cover-Ups, and Conspiracies He Exposed*. New York: Skyhorse, 2013.

K. Jaishanker — *Cyber Criminology: Exploring Internet Crimes and Criminal Behavior*. Boca Raton, FL: CRC Press, 2011.

George K. Kostopoulos — *Cyberspace and Cybersecurity*. Boca Raton, FL: CRC Press, 2013.

Sara L. Latta — *Cybercrime: Data Trails Do Tell Tales*. Berkeley Heights, NJ: Enslow, 2012.

David Leigh and
Luke Harding

Wikileaks: Inside Julian Assange's War on Secrecy. New York: Public Affairs, 2011.

Joseph Menn

Fatal System Error: The Hunt for the New Crime Lords Who Are Bringing Down the Internet. New York: PublicAffairs, 2010.

Kevin Mitnick with
William L. Simon

Ghost in the Wires: My Adventures as the World's Most Wanted Hacker. New York: Little, Brown, 2011.

Denver Nicks

Private: Bradley Manning, Wiki-Leaks, and the Biggest Exposure of Official Secrets in American History. Chicago: Chicago Review Press, 2012.

Parmy Olson

We Are Anonymous: Inside the Hacker World of Lulzsec, Anony-mous, and the Global Cyber Conspiracy. New York: Little, Brown, 2012.

Kevin Poulsen

Kingpin: How One Hacker Took Over the Billion-Dollar Cybercrime Underground. New York: Crown, 2011.

Derek S. Reveron,
ed.

Cyberspace and National Security: Threats, Opportunities, and Power in a Virtual World. Washington, DC: Georgetown University Press, 2012.

Paul Rosenzweig *Cyber Warfare: How Conflicts in Cyberspace Are Challenging America and Changing the World.* Santa Barbara, CA: Praeger, 2012.

Kyle Schurman *Lulzsec.* Los Angeles: Hyperink, 2012.

Index

A

Afghanistan
  non-state insurgency, 166
  Taliban activities, 133, 161
  US activities, 17, 115, 121, 161,
    163, 166
  WikiLeaks concerns with, 116–
    117, 133–135
AGEX (Above Ground
  Experiments), 183
Alexander, Keith, 177
Al-Qaeda, 25, 90, 137, 160–161
Amamou, Slim, 91
Amazon (company), 123, 129,
  161–162
Amos, James, 161
AnonOps.net, 162
Anonymous (hacker group)
  corporate attacks, 100, 160, 164
  denial-of-service attacks, 162
  failures, 162–163
  goals, 79, 99, 163, 164
  hacking tools used by, 78, 98
  HBGary Federal hacked by, 39
  offline component, 102
  problems dealing with, 166
  reasons for hiding, 102
  Ruffin's criticism of, 101
  social media used by, 101
  US aggressive pursuit of, 90
  war on Ohio declared by, 29
Anti-hacking legislation, 16–17
Anti-SOPA campaign, 78–79
Anti-virus programs, 58–60
Arab Spring, 17, 75, 76, 100
Arms race expansion, by the US,
  183–185
Armstrong, Graham, 77–82

Assad, Bashar al-, 75, 76
Assange, Julian
  arrest, 160
  background, 116
  Collateral Murder video and,
    118, 119
  difficulties, 84
  "doomsday" file creation, distri-
    bution, 87
  left-leaning supporters of, 86
  ongoing posts by, 128–129
  potential destruction caused by,
    131
  withdrawal of services to, 85, 87
  See also WikiLeaks
Asymmetric warfare, 164–165
Aurora test, 32
Aweys, Hassan Dahir, 106–107

B

Ba'ath Party, 75
Ball, James, 88–96
Barlow, John Perry, 89, 90
Barnes & Noble, 47
Barrett, Devlin, 37–42
Battle of Britain, 32–33
Bejtlich, Richard, 40
Belarus, 47, 48, 145
Berger, Sandy, 181–182
Besson, Eric, 130
BICEP (Basic Investigation of
  Computers and Electronic
  Crimes) training program, 51
Bitcoins, 89, 93–95
BJ's Wholesale Club, 47
"Black hat" hackers, 16
Bloomberg News security study, 60
Boston Market, 47
Brito, Jerry, 34

Brown, Barrett, 163
Bush, George W., 24, 117
Businesses and companies
    assessment by Henry, Shawn,
        38–42
    congressional protection mea-
        sures, 38
    data breach costs, *40*
    data security breaches, 2011
        and 2012, *156*
    Eastern Europe–based hacking
        scheme, 47–48
    high-profile hacking victims,
        39
    increased hacking activity, 44
    leadership security responsibili-
        ties, 41–42
    private industry cybersecurity
        leadership, 57–62
    private sector security enhance-
        ment, 173
    self-protection, 37–42
    See also Private industry; *indi-
        vidual businesses*
Butler, Lee, 182
Butler, Richard, 181–182

C
Cablegate, 107–108, *135*
Camera/Shy (software), 99–100
Canalys, 58, 60
Carnegie Mellon University, 50,
    54–55
CBS News poll, 122
Center for Strategic and
    International Studies, 28, 39
Central Intelligence Agency (CIA),
    49
CERT Liaison Program (CLP), 50,
    54–55
Chaos Computer Club (Germany),
    16, 98

Chemical Facilities Anti-Terrorism
    Standards (CFATS), 174
China
    citizen information access, 113
    computer capabilities assess-
        ment, 40–41
    credit/debit card hacking
        scheme, 47–48
    Great Firewall of, 99
    hacking of US computers, 41
    rebuffs to the United States,
        133
Chronister, Renee, 64, 65
Church of Scientology, 102
The Citizen Lab (University of
    Toronto), 102
Clapper, James, 172, 177
Clarke, Richard, 155
Climategate scandal, 110, 111
Clinton, Bill, 181–182
Clinton, Hillary Rodham
    documents disclosure descrip-
        tion, 128, 131
    remarks on Internet freedom,
        24, 25
Clinton, Larry, 58
CNET News (website), 99
CNN poll, 122
Cold War
    deterrence strategies, 23
    end of secrecy period, 115–116
    military-industrial complex, 34
    post-war, weapons delivery sys-
        tems, 183
    US strength during, 27
Collaboration, in fighting cyber-
    crime, 26–27, 48–50
Collateral Murder (video), 107,
    118, 119
Command-and-control systems,
    23, 169

Commission on Disarmament
(CD), 181
Comprehensive National
Cybersecurity Initiative, 24
Comprehensive Test Ban Treaty
(CTBT), 181
Computer Forensics (ECSAP-CF)
training program, 52
Computer Fraud and Abuse Act
(1986), 16–17
Constantine, Conrad, 67–72
Council on Europe's Convention
on Cybercrime, 25
Counter Hack Challenges (organi-
zation), 65
Counterinsurgency (COIN) field
manual, 161
Covered critical infrastructure
(CCI) program, 174–175
Craigslist, 79
Credit card fraud schemes, 44–46
Criminal Intelligence Section
(CIS; Secret Service), 50, 54
Critical Infrastructure Protection
Advisory Council (CIPAC), 173
Cult of the Dead Cow (cDc) hack-
ers, 98, 99
"Cyber doom" rhetoric, 34
Cyber sabotage, 128
Cyber Shock Wave simulation,
22
Cyberattacks
2008 attack, 21
against federal networks, 86
as battlefield of the future,
140–142
counterinsurgency vs. cyber-
insurgency, 166–167
cyberspace deterrents of, 150
definition, 154–155
effectiveness, 17

exaggeration of threats by, 155,
157
hacker coordination of, 16
Internet data, 28
investigation of effects, 31–32
military response inappropri-
ateness, 153–158
NetWitness reports data, 22
penetration testing simulation,
19
threat level of, 140
Cybercrime and cybercriminals
complexity of schemes, 47–48
economic threats of, 177
efforts at staying ahead of, 173
global syndicates, 46–47
transnational organizations, 43
CyberCrime and Digital Law
Enforcement Conference, 100
Cyber-industrial complex, emergence of, 34
Cyberinsurgency
counterinsurgency vs., 166–167
need for US strategy, 159–170
strategic elements, 167–170
Cybersecurity
agencies associated with,
157–158
building, in host nations,
169–170
Chamber of Commerce re-
quests for, 41
Cold War lessons, 23
congressional legislation efforts,
37, 38, 41, 58
damage assessment, 33–35
hackers as nonthreatening to,
28–36
importance of collaboration,
26–27, 48–50
multifaceted approaches, 43–56

practical policies, 23–24
preemptive strategies, 25–26
private industry leadership in,
57–62
regulation of, 37, 38, 41, 58
regulation's limitations on,
174–176
risk reduction strategies,
173–174
strategic target identification, 33
technology development, 24–25
threat of deterrence, 35–36
unified approach necessity,
21–27
Cyberwar
as battlefield of the future,
140–142
Cold War lessons, 21
concern of experts about, 17
global declaration of, 128–129
implications for, 163–165
rise of, 162–163
threat exaggerations, 29–30
treaty talks recommendations,
180–185

D
Data mining, 55
Data warehousing, 55
Dave & Buster's, 47
Defending a New Domain (Lynn),
59
Defense Advanced Research
Projects Agency (DARPA), 177
Deibert, Ron, 102–103
Denial-of-service (DoS) attacks,
16, 17, 30
Denning, Dorothy E., 14
Department of Defense Cyber
Strategy, 29
Distributed Denial of Service
(DDoS) attacks, 78, 98, 100–101

Document dropping, 81
Dominguez, Ricardo, 101, 102
Domscheit-Berg, Daniel, 118, 119,
120
Drake, Thomas, 111, 113
Drug Enforcement
Administration, International
Organized Crime and
Intelligence Operations Center,
49

E
Eastern Europe, 47–48, 184
Eggers, Matthew, 41
Eisenhower, Dwight D., 27
Electrical power plants, 38
Electronic bulletin boards, 16
Electronic Crimes Special Agent
Program (ECSAP), 44, 50–52
Electronic Crimes Task Force
(ECTF), 44, 52–53, 58
Electronic Disturbance Theater
(EDT), 101–102
Electronic Frontiers Foundation
(EFF), 89
Ellsberg, Daniel, 134
See also Pentagon Papers
Elmore, Phil, 83–87
Estonia, 30, 47–48
Ethical hackers and hacking
alternate names, 19, 63
argument against legitimizing,
72
benefits of using, 63
debate about hiring, 68
defined, 64
historical background, 19–20
insight provided by, 65–66
as perpetual problem-solving,
64–65
Ethical hacking certificates, 71
Ethicality of hacktivism, 79–81

Europol (European Police Office), 49

EveryDNS.net, 123, 130

F

Facebook
  Arab Spring posts on, 17, 75–76
  DDoS attacks through, 162
  human rights promotions on, 101

Falkvinge, Rickard, 91

Farmer, Dan, 20

FBI (Federal Bureau of Investigation)
  cyber threat warnings, 177
  hacking investigation data, 16, 38
  Joint Terrorism Task Forces (JTTF), 49
  power limitations in other countries, 85
  security recommendations, 41
  stolen data discoveries, 39–40
  terrorism task forces, 49

Federal Communications Commission (FCC), 178

Federal Energy Regulatory Commission-North American Reliability Corporation Critical Information Protection (FERC-NERC CIP), 174

Financial Crimes Enforcement Network (FinCEN), 49

Fleming, John Ambrose, 14–15

FloodNet, 101, 102

Friedman, Benjamin H., 153–158

Fukushima (Japan) nuclear disaster, 69, 185

G

Gates, Robert, 133

Georgia, 30, 182

Germany
  enforcement collaboration, 48
  hacker coalitions, 16, 98
  hacking law, 71
  hacktivism activity, 91

Global syndicate of cybercriminals, 46–47

Google, 22, 26, 80, 133

Gorecki, Eddie, 78

Government-associated hackers, 17

Gramm-Leach Bliley Act (GLBA), 174

Guantanamo Bay detention camp (Cuba), 107, 110, 111

The Guardian (newspaper), 107, 115, 116, 120

Guerilla cyberwarfare, rise of, 162–163

H

Hackers
  cyberattack coordination, 16
  government-associated, 17
  hiring decisions, 71
  implication of principles, 95–96
  last resort use of, 81–82
  mindset, 69
  as nonthreatening to cybersecurity, 28–36
  redefining, 68–69
  term connotations of, 68
  term derivation, 15
  See also Ethical hackers and hacking; Hacktivism; Hacktivists and hacktivist collectives

Hackers: Heroes of the Computer Revolution (Levy), 14

Hacktivism
  Arab Spring role, 76
  defined, 75, 78

Deibert, Ron, studies of, 102–103

effectiveness/ethicality in social protest, 77–82

emergence of, 17

free speech abridged by, 97–103

growing awareness of in US, 85

myth of, 85–87

national security threat status, 87

scrutinizing the effectiveness of, 78–79

on social media sites, 17, 76, 162

Syrian Civil War and, 76

Hacktivism, From Here to There (Ruffin), 100

Hacktivismo (hacker group), 99–100

Hacktivists and hacktivist collectives

fight for civil liberties, free expression, 88–96

goals, 89–90

increasing political involvement, 91–92

motivations, 17, 88

potential attack against Wiki-Leaks, 130–131

Syrian war involvement, 75, 76

targets of attacks by, 81

terrorist status, 83–87

See also Anonymous (hacking collective); WikiLeaks

Harding, Luke, 116

Hayward, John, 57–62

HBGary Federal, 39

Health Insurance Portability and Accountability Act (HIPAA), 174

Helicopter video (April 2010). *See Collateral Murder* (video)

Henry, Shawn, 38–42

HUMINT (human intelligence) strategies, 167–168

I

Idaho National Labs, 32

Imperialism (Lenin), 135

Indian Coalition for Nuclear Disarmament and Peace, 181

Information brokerage, 55

Inside WikiLeaks (Domscheit-Berg), 118

Intellectual property protection efforts, 80, 92

Intelligence Community (US), 152

Intercontinental ballistic missiles, 23

International Strategy for Cyber-space (Obama administration), 149

Internet

Bitcoin currency, 89, 93–95

free speech protections, 90–91

increasing usage of, 19

need for strengthened security, 25

open Internet, benefits of, 92–93

Usenet forum, 20

Internet Security Alliance, 58

INTERPOL (International Criminal Police Office), 49

Iran

arming of China and North Korea and, 134

cyberattack accusations against United States, 146

global sanctions against, 145

Operation Iran, 97, 100–101

potential limited deterrence strategy, 35

Stuxnet nuclear facility cyber-attack, 29–32, 131, 146

Taliban armed by, 133
war against "the Great Satan"
by, 140
Iraq
al-Qaeda operatives in, 25, 90,
137, 160–161
hacktivist interventions against,
17, 98
non-state insurgency in, 166
US activities in, 161
WikiLeaks disclosures on, 117,
119
Is This the Start of CyberWar?
(Weinberger), 141

J
The Jester (hacker), 79, 130
Johnson, Lyndon B., administra-
tion, 134
Joint Terrorism Task Forces
(JTTF), 49
Judis, John B., 132–137

K
Karg, Dominique, 67–72
Katrina (hurricane), 33
Keller, Bill, 125
Kennedy, John F., 134
Kenya, citizen access to informa-
tion, 113

L
L0pht (hacker group), 98
Lambda Labs, 64
Lanchester, John, 118
Law Enforcement agencies (US),
152
Legion of Doom (hacker group), 16
Legions of the Underground
(hacker group), 98
Leigh, David, 116, 120
Levin, Carl, 34, 155
Levy, Steven, 14

Lewis, James Andrew, 28–36, 38
Lewman, Andrew, 92–93
Lieberman, Joe, 90, 130
Los Alamos National Laboratory,
16, 183
*Loving the Cyber Bomb? The
Dangers of Threat Inflation in
Cybersecurity Policy* (Brito and
Watkins), 34
Low Orbit Ion Cannon (LOIC), 78
LulzSec (online group), 79, 89
Lynn, William J., III, 59, 167

M
Manning, Bradley, 110–111, 113,
124, 139
Marconi, Guglielmo, 14–15
Maskelyne, Nevil, 15
Massachusetts Institute of
Technology, 15
Mastercard, 87, 90, 123, 160, 162
May, Cliff, 138–141
McAfee, 58–60
McConnell, Mike, 21–27, 140, 141,
155
McOmie, Luke, 64
Megaupload.com, 89
Merritt, Michael P., 43–56
Microsoft Windows, 98, 145, 168
Middle East
Arab Spring, 17, 75, 76, 100
Britain's withdrawal from, 132
pro-democracy movements,
17, 75
Sykes-Picot agreement, 134,
135, 136–137
WikiLeaks information about,
106, 135
See also Iran; Iraq
Mills, Elinor, 97–103
Mitnick, Kevin, 70, 71
Le Monde (newspaper), 107, 115

Moore, Michael, 85, 86, 87
Moore's law, 59
Morse code, 14
MP3 file sharing, 113
Mueller, Robert, 177

N
Napster, 113
Nasdaq, 39
National Archives (US), 117
National Computer Forensics Institute (NCFI), 44, 53–54
National Cyber Investigative Joint Task Force (NCIJTF), 49
National Cyber Security Division (US-CERT), 49, 168–169
National Infrastructure Protection Plan (NIPP), 173
National Intelligence Program, 172, 177
National Press Club (Washington, DC), 118
National Protection and Program Directorate (NPPD), 49
National Public Radio, 85
National Security Agency (NSA)
    Alexander, Keith, leadership role, 177
    charges against whistleblowers, 111
    cyber operation activities, 152, 157
    harnessing the abilities of, 26
    McConnell, Mike, leadership role, 140
    responsibilities of, 26
National Security Council (NSC), 49
National Security Strategy (US), 167, 168
National Security Task Force (US), 172

NATO (North Atlantic Treaty Organization), 23
NetWitness, 22
Network Intrusion Responder (ECSAP), 50–52, 55
New York City–based credit card fraud scheme, 45
New York Times (newspaper), 107, 115, 125, 134
North Africa, pro-democracy protests, 75
Nuclear reactors, 38

O
Obama, Barack, administration
    choice to not use hackers, 130
    double standards of, 110–111
    hacking of, 76, 110–111
    International Strategy for Cyberspace, 149
    Iran hacking by, 146
    National Security Strategy, 167, 168
    WikiLeaks condemned by, 133
O'Brien, Chris, 85
Occupy movement, 80, 89, 98, 102
Occupy the Vote (political movement), 98
Office of Investigations (US Secret Service), 43
OfficeMax, 47
Online banking, 25, 154
Operation Iran website, 97, 100–101
Operation Payback, 81, 162
Oxblood Ruffin (hacker), 99, 100–101

P
El País (newspaper), 107, 115
PayPal, 87, 90, 123, 130, 160, 162
Payroll company fraud scheme, 45
Peer-to-peer sites, 80

Pentagon Papers, 116, 121, 132, 134
Petraeus, David, 161
PIPA (Protect Intellectual Property Act), 80
Pirate Bay (website), 80
Pirate Party, 89
Ponemon Institute, 60
Poremba, Sue Marquette, 63–66
Preble, Christopher, 153–158
Presidential Directive No. 7 (HSPD-7), 173
Private industry
cybersecurity leadership role, 57–62
dynamism of, 59
security enhancements, 173
security-related legal liability issues, 61
use of anti-virus programs, 58–60
See also Businesses and companies; *individual businesses*
Project Chanology, 102
Project Solarium, 22, 27
Protect Intellectual Property Act (PIPA), 80

R
Red teams (ethical hackers), 19
Reddit, 79
Reddy, Amulya, 183
Reuters, 107, 110, 115, 119
Ridge, Tom, 171–179
Roberts, Alasdair, 114–126
Rockefeller, Jay, 155
Rosenzweig, Paul, 159–170

S
SANS Institute, 65
Sarbanes-Oxley (SOX) Act, 174
ScatterChat, 100
Science and Technology Directorate (S&T), 49

Secret Service. *See* US Secret Service
Security Administrator Tool for Analyzing Networks (SATAN), 20
Security Pacific Bank, 16
Skoudis, Ed, 65–66
Slater, Alice, 180–185
Small Biz Cyber Planner, 178
Sneakers (ethical hackers), 19
Software Engineering Institute (SEI), 54
Sony Corporation, 39
SOPA (Stop Online Piracy Act), 78, 79, 80, 91
Spain, 48, 107, 182
Der Spiegel (newspaper), 107, 115, 117
Sports Authority, 47
Stanesby, Jonathan, 78
"Stockpile stewardship" program, 182, 183
Stop Online Piracy Act (SOPA), 78, 79, 80, 91
Strategic Command (Pentagon), 157
Stuxnet virus
attack on Iran nuclear facilities, 29–32, 131, 141, 146
real-world effects of, 165
Symantec analysis of, 145–146
US government involvement, 146–147, 157
VirusBlokAda's identification of, 141, 145
Sykes-Picot agreement (1916), 134, 135, 136–137
Symantec, 58–60, 145–146
Syrian Civil War, 17, 75, 76
Syrian Electronic Army, 75, 76

T
3D printers, 95

Taaki, Amir, 95, 96
Taliban, 133, 161
Tendell, Charles, 65
Thiessen, Marc A., 127–131
Tiger teams (ethical hackers), 19
TJX Companies, 47, 48
Tor (software), 100
Transborder Immigrant Tool,
　101–102
Tunisia, pro-democracy protests,
　75, 100
Turkey, 48
Twitter
　Arab Spring posts on, 17, 75–
　76
　DDoS attacks through, 162
　human rights promotions on,
　101

U
Ukraine, 45, 48
United Arab Emirates, 48
United States
　activities in Afghanistan, 17,
　115, 121, 161, 163, 166
　arms race expansion by,
　183–185
　China's hacking computers in,
　41
　confrontation of serious cyber-
　threats, 151–152
　cyberattacks against federal net-
　works, *86*
　cybersecurity awareness cam-
　paign, *178*
　credit/debit card hacking
　scheme, 47–48
　cyberspace counterinsurgency
　needs, 159–170
　cyberwar losses, 22
　cyberwar treaty talk promotion,
　180–185

Google-government partner-
　ship, 26
government regulation limita-
　tions, 171–179
hacktivism, awareness of, 85
Legions of the Underground
　and, 98
nuclear arsenal safety, 182–183
security spending recommen-
　dation, 60–62
WikiLeaks and, 124, 127–131,
　138–142
See also specific agencies,
　presidential administrations,
　and listings beginning with
　"National"
United States Cyber Command
　(USCYBERCOM), 152
US Chamber of Commerce, 41,
　172–179
US Congress
　anti-hacking legislation, 16–17
　challenges maintaining vigi-
　lance, 175
　cybersecurity legislation efforts,
　37, 38, 41, 58
　intellectual property protection
　efforts, 80
　need for information-sharing
　bill, 178–179
　Public Law 107-56, 52
US Department of Defense (DoD)
　Cyber Strategy, 29
　on dynamism of private indus-
　try, 59
　five pillars of cyber strategy,
　167–168
　hacking of computer system of,
　141–142
　on military response to cyber-
　attacks, 148–152

US Department of Homeland
Security
CCI program regulation,
174–175
Chamber of Commerce advo-
cacy for, 176
cyberalarm budget, 157
Cybersecurity Act authorization
of, 174
entities/non-entities related to,
49, 150–151
partnerships, 53, 56, 178
Presidential Directive No. 7
(HSPD-7), 172, 173
Science and Technology
Directorate (S&T), 49
virus threat level indicator, 60
White House staff, 49
US Department of Justice, 78
US Drug Enforcement
Administration (DEA), 49
US House of Representatives
Energy and Commerce sub-
committee, 58
US Secret Service
BICEP training program, 51
CERT Liaison Program, 50,
54–55
credit card fraud identification,
44–46
Criminal Intelligence Section,
50, 54
ECSAP-CF training program,
52
ECSAP-NI training program,
51–52
ECTF's established by, 52–53
Electronic Crimes Task Forces,
44
global offices, 54
international collaborations, 54

multifaceted approach, 49–50
Office of Investigations, 43
three-year cybercrime investi-
gation, 48
US Senate Armed Services
Committee, 34
US Senate Homeland Security
and Governmental Affairs
Committee, 130, 177
US Single Integrated Operations
Plan, 33
US State Department, 115, 117,
121, 123, 133
US Treasury Department, 49
Usenet, 20

V
Venema, Wietse, 20
VirusBlokAda, 141, 145
Visa (company), 81, 87, 90, 123

W
Walker, Jesse, 109–113
Wall Street Journal (newspaper),
154
War Games (movie), 16
Washington Post (newspaper), 134
Watkins, Tate, 34
Weinberger, Sharon, 141
"White hats" (hackers), 16, 19, 98
WikiLeaks
Afghan war documents release,
120
assault on state authority by,
161–162
assessment of impact of,
116–117
Cablegate, 107, 108, 135
Climategate scandal, 110, 111
Collateral Murder (video) and,
107, 119
counterinsurgency manuals re-
lease, 118

criticisms of, 111–112
cutting off of, 123–124
dangers related to, 83
description, 110–111, 112
destabilizing impact of, 122
fights against, 129–130
flawed mission, 118
foreign policy role, 132–137
goals, 106
Guantanamo prison manual,
    107, 110, 111
hacktivist potential efforts
    against, 130–131
hyperbole related to, 29
information distribution dis-
    ruption, 123
initial attention given to,
    106–107
key partnerships, 120–121
lack of control of hackers by, 87
Manning, Bradley, leaks to,
    110–111, 113
national security threatened by,
    127–131
newspapers agreements, 107,
    115

open secrets released by,
    125–126
problems with, 124–125
risk assessments, 112–113
romanticisim of hacktivism by,
    84
scandal leaks consequences,
    114–126
supporters of, 85
topic of debates about, 106
topics discussed in leaked
    cables, *135*
transparency provided by,
    109–113
US government response, 124,
    138–142
US spying statement by,
    107–108
war on secrecy by, 115–116
See also Assange, Julian
Wikipedia, 79
Winfrey, Oprah, 76
Wired (magazine), 155
Wireless telegraph, 14–15
WorldNetDaily (website), 83, 84

CPSIA information can be obtained
at www.ICGtesting.com
Printed in the USA
FFOW01n1007081113
2300FF

9 780737 766578